SAGE was founded in 1965 by Sara Miller McCune to support the dissemination of usable knowledge by publishing innovative and high-quality research and teaching content. Today, we publish over 900 journals, including those of more than 400 learned societies, more than 800 new books per year, and a growing range of library products including archives, data, case studies, reports, and video. SAGE remains majority-owned by our founder, and after Sara's lifetime will become owned by a charitable trust that secures our continued independence.

Los Angeles | London | New Delhi | Singapore | Washington DC

QUALITY AND LEADERSHIP in the Early Years

Research, Theory and Practice

VERITY CAMPBELL-BARR
and CAROLINE LEESON

SAGE

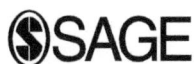

Los Angeles | London | New Delhi
Singapore | Washington DC

Los Angeles | London | New Delhi
Singapore | Washington DC

SAGE Publications Ltd
1 Oliver's Yard
55 City Road
London EC1Y 1SP

SAGE Publications Inc.
2455 Teller Road
Thousand Oaks, California 91320

SAGE Publications India Pvt Ltd
B 1/I 1 Mohan Cooperative Industrial Area
Mathura Road
New Delhi 110 044

SAGE Publications Asia-Pacific Pte Ltd
3 Church Street
#10-04 Samsung Hub
Singapore 049483

Editor: Amy Jarrold
Assistant editor: George Knowles
Production editor: Nicola Marshall
Copyeditor: Sharon Cawood
Indexer: Silvia Benvenuto
Marketing manager: Dilhara Attygalle
Cover designer: Wendy Scott
Typeset by: C&M Digitals (P) Ltd, Chennai, India
Printed and bound by
CPI Group (UK) Ltd, Croydon, CR0 4YY

© Verity Campbell-Barr and Caroline Leeson, 2016

First published 2016

Apart from any fair dealing for the purposes of research or private study, or criticism or review, as permitted under the Copyright, Designs and Patents Act, 1988, this publication may be reproduced, stored or transmitted in any form, or by any means, only with the prior permission in writing of the publishers, or in the case of reprographic reproduction, in accordance with the terms of licences issued by the Copyright Licensing Agency. Enquiries concerning reproduction outside those terms should be sent to the publishers.

Library of Congress Control Number: 2015941031

British Library Cataloguing in Publication data

A catalogue record for this book is available from the British Library

ISBN 978-1-4739-0647-1
ISBN 978-1-4739-0648-8 (pbk)

At SAGE we take sustainability seriously. Most of our products are printed in the UK using FSC papers and boards. When we print overseas we ensure sustainable papers are used as measured by the PREPS grading system. We undertake an annual audit to monitor our sustainability.

CONTENTS

List of Figures and Tables	viii
Acknowledgements	ix
About the Authors	x

Introduction	**1**
Our Parameters	3
The Book	4
PART ONE QUALITY	**9**
1 Why an Interest in Quality?	**11**
Who Has an Interest in Quality Early Years Services?	12
Global Interests	12
European Interests	15
Why the Interest in Quality Early Years Services?	16
Hegemonic Views of Early Years Services	19
Cultural Interpretations of Early Years Services	21
Modernist Approaches to Quality	22
Post-structuralist Approaches to Quality	25
Further Reading	27
2 What is Quality? Exploring the Evidence Base	**28**
Quality Frameworks	28
Quality Outside the Rating Scales Box	32
The Panoptic Gaze	34
Parental Perspectives on Quality	36
The Early Years Market and Parental Choice	38
Child Views on Quality	40
Your Views on Quality	42
Further Reading	44

PART TWO LEADERSHIP — 45

3 Tracing the Development of Early Years Leadership — 47
Early Experiences of Leadership in Early Years Settings — 48
Influential Leadership Theories — 50
The New Leadership Paradigm — 55
Entrepreneurial Leadership — 58
Conclusion — 60
Further Reading — 62

4 Early Years Leaders – All Things to All People — 63
The Many Accountabilities of Early Years Leaders — 63
The Many Titles of Early Years Leaders — 76
The Many Jobs of Early Years Leaders — 80
The Activist Leader — 80
Further Reading — 82

PART THREE IMPLICATIONS FOR PRACTICE — 83

Our Practitioners — 84
Jacky — 85
Sue — 85
Sandra — 85
Cheryl — 85
The Writing Framework — 86

5 Visions of Quality — 89
Your Vision of Quality — 90
The Interplay of Structural and Process Features of Quality — 93
Staffing — 98
Qualifications — 100
Your Principles Based on the Needs of the Child — 101
Further Reading — 104

6 Reflecting on Leading Quality Early Years Services — 105
Models of Reflection — 108
Reflective Accounts of Leadership Challenge — 110
The Importance of Emotional Well-being for Leaders — 110
Working in Partnership with Parents — 114
The Interrelatedness of Principles and Action — 117
Engaging the Team in Reflective Activity — 120
Reflective Themes — 122
Why Would You Not Want Reflective Leaders? — 125
Further Reading — 126

Conclusion **127**
    External Forces on Understandings of the Early Years   128
    How Might Settings Respond to the Communities in Which
    They are Located?   131

Glossary   135
References   137
Index   150

LIST OF FIGURES AND TABLES

Figures

2.1 Aspects of quality early years provision 43

4.1 The critical role of the leader 64
4.2 Management (procedure led) and leadership (process led) tasks within an early years setting 79

6.1 Sue's Jigsaw 120

Tables

3.1 Table of leadership theory 51

ACKNOWLEDGEMENTS

We would like to acknowledge the hard work and commitment of the four practitioners – Cheryl, Jacky, Sandra and Sue – whose work in their settings is inspiring. Our time spent together in discussion and debate was uplifting and instructive with lots of opportunity to learn from each other.

We would also like to thank Amy Jarrold for her support and commitment to our project and her encouraging comments throughout the writing process.

Last, but by no means least, we wish to thank our families: Matt and Reuben, and Ian, Rob and Josh, who provide the important grounding for all the work we do.

ABOUT THE AUTHORS

Verity Campbell-Barr is a lecturer in Early Childhood Studies at Plymouth University where she teachers on both undergraduate and postgraduate courses. She has extensive research experience in early childhood education and care (ECEC) policy, considering concepts of value for money, the reliance on the market in services provision and the role of ECEC in welfare-to-work reforms. Her core interest lies in the quality of ECEC services and particularly the role of the workforce in delivering quality provision. She has recently completed research on the quality of early years services for 2-year-olds in England and a European project on the attitudinal competences advocated for early childhood practitioners. She is about to embark on a research project to explore the knowledge, skills and attitudes required of ECEC practitioners across Europe within the context of the quality of provision. Her research experience and time spent in practice make her a true believer in the need for the voice of ECEC practitioners as the true experts in policy formation.

Caroline Leeson is an associate professor in Early Childhood Studies at Plymouth University. She has particular interests in the welfare of looked-after children, children's centre leadership and reflective practice and enjoys working with students towards their goal of being strong advocates for young children and their families. Her research interests are in social justice; children with a parent in prison; children who go missing and/or are vulnerable to sexual exploitation; and the involvement of children in decision-making processes. She is also active in researching the articulation of leadership in early years settings. Before working in higher education, she was a social worker in child protection, fostering and adoption and the leader of a family centre for a period of time. This experience proved particularly profound as she learnt the importance of communication, collaboration and the joy of spending time in the home corner making stone soup.

INTRODUCTION

To want quality early years services that are effectively led appears common sense for any society that wants children to have good quality experiences. It is perhaps unsurprising then that there is such an interest in quality and leadership in the early years. Given that quality and leadership are so important to early years services, you would think that they would be easily understood, yet quality and leadership are two words that are frequently used but rarely defined. **Supranational organisations** (see Glossary for words in bold) such as the European Union talk about the importance of quality early years services – in fact, they have priorities in regard to improving the quality of early years provision, but a definition of quality is much harder to come by. Equally, when looking at leadership, there is a great deal of commentary as to the desirability of effective leadership to lead high quality settings with some indication of how that leadership might be articulated. However, a clear definition of what leadership looks like and what leaders do, is currently unavailable, meaning that there is often an understanding of what poor leadership is, but not of what good leadership looks like. The difficulty in forming an understanding of both quality and leadership in the early years is something that we will explore in detail in the coming chapters, but we also want to explore the interrelationship between quality and leadership. It has always come as a surprise to us that there is little that explores this relationship. We are aware that often leadership is seen as a feature of quality early years provision, but what this actually means theoretically or practically is not explored. In some ways, there is something of a chicken-and-egg debate – do you need good leaders to achieve good quality or does good quality create good leadership? But in considering this conundrum, we can begin to see the complexities that lie ahead in exploring these two terms. Not only is it about exploring what quality and leadership are, but it is also about what 'good' means.

In this book, we aim to explore the meanings and understandings of quality and leadership that are present in early years services. We consider how both quality and leadership are complex, multifaceted and contested terms, but we view this as presenting early years practice with opportunities. We hope that in exploring quality and leadership and the ways in which both terms have been conceptualised from a range of different perspectives, you will be able to find a meaning that is right for you and your practice. We view both quality and leadership as fluid and dynamic terms – the understanding that you create today may well be different from that which you create next week, next month or next year. This is because we believe that quality and leadership are relative terms – most specifically, they relate to the context that they are in, so (as we will explore in Chapters 1 and 3) whilst there is a global interest in these terms, this does not mean that there is a global definition – far from it.

In the book, we are influenced by **post-structuralism**, whereby we believe that it is important to consider what and who is shaping understandings of quality and leadership, and that settings should be jointly constructing a shared understanding from within settings of quality and leadership. Some of the critiques that we present in this book are based on a view that, all too often, understandings of quality and leadership are not constructed in collaboration with early years practitioners. Indeed, frequently early years practitioners can be objectified in the process to formulate an understanding of quality and leadership. The result is that often there are technocratic definitions, intended to guide practice but frequently feeling restrictive in the advice that they offer. For this reason, we draw on post-structuralist perspectives as we feel these are helpful in enabling us to break down the structures that objectify us. They allow us to see that there is no one definition of quality or leadership and that there are multiple ways of leading quality early years provision. To this end, the book is intended to support you in developing *your* understanding of quality and how you would like to lead this. This is where social constructionism also influences us, as we believe that understandings of quality and leadership should be constructed to reflect your social context, so that they become terms that are meaningful for you and your early years practice. As we lead you through the chapters, we will be asking you to reflect on what you have learnt so that you can formulate your own opinions.

Our Parameters

In this book, we will refer to early years provision as representing those services for children that are not yet of compulsory school age. Our own context is that we are based in England, and thus our understanding of early years provision is those services for children from birth to 5 years of age.

We have chosen this age range because school is compulsory from age 5 in England, and because the curriculum we have in England – the Early Years Foundation Stage (EYFS) – applies to children from birth to 5 years of age. However, we are aware that in other contexts, the understanding of early years services regarding when children are of compulsory school age is different.

In defining early years services as those which deliver the EYFS, we are aware that this in itself is problematic. In looking more closely at those who deliver the EYFS, we can see that there are a range of different providers: day nurseries, pre-schools, children's centres, childminders and so on. Those who deliver the EYFS come from a range of contexts, both in regard to the leadership and management of their settings and the type of services that are on offer. First, considering the leadership and management of settings, those delivering the EYFS can come from the private, voluntary, independent (PVI) and maintained sectors. Even looking within these sectors, there are subtle differences – for example, in the maintained sector there are nursery schools (standalone EYFS providers) and schools that have reception classes or reception units. In fact, most 4-year-olds in England are in school and here the leadership model may not be one sufficiently focused on the early years and its strong emphasis on caring, positive relationships. Equally, in the private sector, there are differences in the size and scale of settings, both in regard to how many children are being catered for and whether the setting is part of a large global chain or a small local one. Just in looking at this wide range, we can see that quality and leadership are going to mean different things to different providers, but we think this is important. Our primary interest in this book is with the PVI sector – currently the largest sector and the one that has been the focus of much of the recent policy development on the leadership of quality early years provision. This policy focus has been based on deficit assumptions that regard the PVI sector as most likely to be lacking in leadership skills, to have poorly qualified staff, the least favourable buildings and structure, and therefore requiring the most remedial action in terms of development, inspection and monitoring in order to support the development of quality. Throughout the book, we take a critical approach to this deficit model, not just in wanting to appreciate the exciting and innovative early years practice that exists, but also in looking to deconstruct the deficit model and its aims and purpose when developing the quality and leadership of early years settings. Quality and leadership should always be relevant to the context that they are in and it is our belief that a one-size-fits-all mentality that tends to underpin policy development in this area is unhelpful to the variety of settings and the very different communities that they serve. As we go through the different chapters, we will talk about early years services generically, but, where needed, we will highlight the differences between the services that are on offer. We draw heavily on our knowledge and understanding of the English context, but we also consider international research on quality and leadership in order to highlight different approaches and ways of thinking. Considering international perspectives can aid the development of an understanding of quality and leadership, but we stress throughout the book that looking at international perspectives and considering examples is about facilitating the development of *your* understanding of quality and leadership, not an attempt to privilege one model over another.

The Book

We begin by outlining the global interest in quality early years services. We look at who are the stakeholders that have an interest in early years services and how they contribute to understandings of the benefits of quality early years services in relation to child outcomes. We consider how the interest in early years services impacts on understandings of quality, including considering how the outcomes that are assessed within early years practice influence how quality is defined. We draw on modernist approaches to highlight how often quality has been framed by what can be measured, but question the desirability of such approaches. We look at how a preoccupation with measurement is part of a global framework that looks to demonstrate the effectiveness of early years provision, and we suggest that such a framework is dominated by human capital perspectives and normative expectations around child development (where there is a focus on the cognitive development of children as a linear progression). In looking to demonstrate the effectiveness of early years provision in relation to cognitive development, a series of discursive truths have emerged that demonstrate not only how the purpose of early years provision has been constructed, but also understandings of quality. As such, these definitions become a set of standards to be achieved because they are associated with the desired outcomes rather than something to be questioned or challenged.

In Chapter 2, we develop our discussion around the development of discursive truths by looking to question understandings of quality. Discursive truths present a particular way of thinking and speaking about early years services. Building on our discussions in Chapter 1, we consider how stakeholders, such as policy makers, look to influence the way in which early years services are understood – creating particular ways of speaking about the early years. However, through drawing on research evidence from practitioners, parents and children, we consider in Chapter 2 how there are many different ways to understand early years services, with varying influences on these understandings. We emphasise in Chapter 2 the importance of considering subjective, value-based and culture-bound understandings of quality and their role in creating quality early years environments that are meaningful to the context. In acknowledging the subjective, we also recognise the importance of reflecting on what and who has shaped understandings of quality early years provision and begin to consider how teams can work together to formulate their own understandings. We consider post-structuralist perspectives due to the role that they play in deconstructing preconceived ideas of quality early years services and in asking questions as to who and what has shaped understandings of quality.

In Chapter 3, we turn our attention to leadership. We consider the historic development of early years provision from the informal, village playgroup run by a committee of parents (usually mothers) and the occasional state-run nursery, often attached to a school and administered by the head teacher, to the current landscape that we outlined above, with many stakeholders providing many different settings. Consequently, a lively **discourse** as to how settings might be led shows a shifting theoretical vista moving from theories espoused by the business community, through those developed by a large literature of school leadership towards a unique set of understandings of leadership that firmly belong in the early years sector. In doing so, we recognise the highly feminised concept of early years work, workers and leaders, and debate its significance and influence on the development of models of leadership that place relationships at the centre of leadership activities and offer early years leaders the guidance they need towards the leadership they espouse. We also discuss the recent move towards models of entrepreneurial leadership assisted by the drive towards doing more for less in straitened economic circumstances and a government preference for business models of leadership with 'superhero' charismatic individuals at the helm. Thus, a thorough examination of leadership styles and models from both national and international perspectives will be an integral aspect of this chapter as we seek to identify the various leadership discourses that have developed, and debate their helpfulness or otherwise to the provision of quality services for children and their families.

In Chapter 4, we consider in more depth the challenges that are present for leaders of early years settings in relation to research evidence. Over the last ten years, we have seen considerable development, not only in the affirmation of what should constitute effective models of early years leadership, but also in the provision of services for young children and their families and the expectations on those services (Nutbrown, 2012). All early years workers (not just leaders) are positioned as essential to the successful delivery of early years provision and regarded as central characters within policy delivery (Osgood, 2012). As a consequence of this increased focus on the practice of early years leaders and workers, there has been considerable research into what are the most effective models of leadership. In this chapter, we build on what we have discussed in Chapter 3 to consider the implications of models of leadership on the day-to-day roles and responsibilities of leaders, the many hats that they are required to wear and the many **accountabilities** that they hold, as well as debating the consequences of a lack of distinction between 'leadership' and 'management' and the balance of these often opposing roles within the workplace (McDowall Clark and Murray, 2012). Thus, we explore the impact of current frameworks for accountability, inspection and self-evaluation on the role of the leader and on the identification of effective models of leadership. We also consider the interplay between the focus on up-skilling the workforce and the role of qualifications in developing leadership skills. A further topic for debate will be the concerns raised in research studies about the increased commodification, identity and performance of emotional labour within emotionally intensive environments (Madrid and Dunn-Kenney, 2010).

Having considered understandings of quality and leadership and the evidence that is available for both, we draw things together by thinking about leading quality in a practical way. In Chapter 5, we present four case studies to explore the understanding and articulation of leadership and of developing quality provision in different settings. The case studies have been written in conjunction with early years providers who have a range of working environments and perspectives, and who all have valuable experiences and insights that they have kindly shared with us and therefore you. We provide an overview of our case studies, so that you, the reader, can consider them in context. In Chapter 5, we consider the features of quality early years provision that each of the four case studies chose to focus on. In exploring their understandings of quality, we return to the concept of post-structuralism that we first began to explore in Chapter 2 and that we have linked to throughout the book. We discuss the process of deconstructing our understandings of quality in order to appreciate what has informed them. However, we do not wish this deconstruction to be a negative process, whereby there is nothing left of the understandings at the end. Rather, we explore how reflection and deconstruction can help in developing our understandings of quality and how taking a critical approach does not mean that we have to reject the ideas of policy makers and/or theorists. Instead, we can draw on the understanding of others to aid the reflective process and an understanding of our own thinking. In Chapter 6, we build on this reflective process by considering in more detail the role of reflective practice for developing understandings of quality, whilst also considering the different leadership styles that can be adopted in formulating and articulating quality early years services. In Chapter 6, our case studies present challenges that the practitioners have encountered and discuss the role of reflection in working through those challenges. In particular, the chapter highlights how providers find themselves having to negotiate between competing perspectives of quality from policy, staff, parents and children. The reflections are designed not only to offer you an insight into the thoughts of our case study practitioners on quality and leadership, but also to act as a model for you in developing your own reflective practice through an exploration of the different ways in which that might happen.

In the final chapter, we review the contents of the book. The chapter is broken down into two key areas that we develop throughout the book, the first of which considers the external forces that seek to shape understandings of quality and leadership, while the second deals with responding to the communities in which the settings are located. We do not dispute the importance of quality and leadership, but we wish to highlight that there is more than one interpretation of quality and leadership. As such, the final chapter acts as a reminder of the many competing stakeholders who have an interest in the quality and leadership of early years settings and the varying ways in which they look to shape and define what is quality early years provision and how it should be led. We therefore conclude with a discussion on how, as a leader, you are expected to be able to negotiate between these different elements and on how training, experience and personal disposition all impact on the ability to do this successfully. In the conclusion, we return to what we have outlined here in our introduction – despite the many forms of quality and leadership, what is important is finding an approach that is meaningful to you and the context that you work in. What we aim to do in this book is to support you in considering what and who have shaped your understandings of quality and leadership so that you can articulate your understanding.

We want to conclude that the development of your own understanding of quality and leadership offers significant opportunities for you and your practice. Often, we can feel constrained or bogged down by imposed understandings of both quality and leadership, but we hope that in reading this book you will feel that they are in fact liberating terms – it just depends on how you look at them.

PART ONE
QUALITY

WHY AN INTEREST IN QUALITY?

Chapter Overview

In this chapter, we consider who has an interest in the quality of early years services and why. We look at how the interest in quality early years services spans the globe. This global interest is reflected in how global organisations advocate the importance of early years services and how individual countries look to invest in quality early years services. We consider that, whether contemplating the interest in quality early years as a global issue or a country-level one, the interest in quality will be shaped by views on the role of early years services. We therefore discuss the relationship between quality early years services and child outcomes and parental employment. The role and purpose of early years services will reflect cultural values around children, childhood and family life. We show that it is important to recognise what shapes understandings of quality early years services in order to recognise that there is no one understanding.

Globally, it seems that it is not possible to talk of early years services without prefixing it with the term quality. Quality is a term commonly used by those with an interest in early years services, but why is it that they are so interested in *quality* early years services above and beyond just early years services? At first, you might think, 'why wouldn't you want quality?' and we would agree that this is true; of course we want quality experiences for children, so quality early years environments are going to be a part of this. However, what we hope to trace in this chapter is how the interest in quality influences how it is understood, how it is defined and what this means in practice. Quality is not just a desirable feature, it is a political tool, a value-laden term that seeks to shape understandings as to the purpose of early years services and what they should look like. In this chapter, we identify who it is that has an interest in the quality of early years services, from the global to the local. We look at why there is an interest in the early years and how reasons for that interest impact on understandings of quality. We frame the discussion in relation to *modern* and *post-structuralist* perspectives of quality to provide a critical framework for the consideration of what quality is (as discussed in the next chapter).

Who Has an Interest in Quality Early Years Services?

When considering who it is that has an interest in the quality of early years services, it is evident that there are a number of stakeholders: children, parents, practitioners, managers, leaders, local government, national government and supranational organisations (Cottle and Alexander, 2012). These stakeholders represent both individuals, such as the individual child, and groups, such as a global organisation or a community group of parents. At both the individual and collective levels, the reasons for an interest will be motivated by different concerns, beliefs and perspectives and these will have a bearing on the understandings of quality. Equally, the different perspectives can often overlap and interplay with one another, in turn having implications for practice. Through this chapter and into the next, we look at understandings of quality from the perspectives of the range of stakeholders involved. Our starting point is a consideration of the global interest in early years services, before going on to consider the national (UK) perspective, with the next chapter focusing on the views of practitioners, parents and children.

Global Interests

Supranational organisations refer to those organisations that transcend international borders, such as the World Bank, the OECD, Unicef and the European Union. Each of these organisations offers advice and guidance to individual countries on a number of policy areas, not just on early years. The last 20 to 30 years have seen a number of supranational organisations promote the idea that individual countries should not only provide early years services, but should also invest in them to ensure that they are of a high quality. The extent of the advice and guidance varies as does the extent to which national governments have to act on it, but what we are interested in here is the global messages that are being disseminated pertaining to the importance of quality early years services.

As an organisation, the Organisation for Economic Co-operation and Development (OECD) identifies its mission as being 'to promote policies that will improve the economic and social well-being of people around the world' (OECD, no date). It sees itself as providing a forum for countries to share their approach on numerous policy areas, including early years. Whilst this presents a collaborative approach, organisations such as the OECD have a strong influence on global ideas around policy making. The OECD has published three systematic reviews into early years provision that have considered the question of what quality is – the Starting Strong series (OECD, 2001, 2006, 2011, 2015). In addition, the OECD has carried out a number of country reviews that provide comprehensive overviews of early years services in the respective countries. Prior to the publication of the first Starting Strong report, the OECD outlined a commitment to improving the access to and quality of early childhood education and care (Bennett, 2006). The reports involved systematic reviews of countries in terms of the delivery of early years services and the policy structures (and investments) that supported these. The reviews were then able to create an understanding of successful features on a range of areas relating to early years services from investment in services to pedagogy (how practitioners work with children) and parental partnerships (Bennett, 2006).

The interest in early years services by the OECD reflects the dual policy agendas of supporting parental employment and recognising the early years as an important foundation for later lifelong learning. These two rationales for investing in early years services are now characteristic of much early years policy making in many countries. First, the overall supply of early years services will help to ensure that parents who choose to can use early years services to support employment opportunities. This is key to equality agendas as it is primarily about ensuring that women are not hindered in accessing the labour market as a result of family commitments, thus placing them on an equal footing with men. This is not to say that men do not take on family responsibilities, but gender norms still prevail in the managing of work–life balance in many households (Lewis et al., 2008). Equally, we recognise that the provision of early years services is not the only factor in determining access to employment. There will be structural features, such as the cost of care, opening hours, location and so on that will influence the use of services, as well as preferential features, such as opting to stay at home to care for children. Support for parental employment entwines with the second aspect of investing in early years services: child development. Accepting that early years services support child development, the provision of early years services ensures equality of access to those developmental advantages for all children. Quality is an important feature in both of these agendas. In telling parents that early years services support child development, it acts as a persuasive mechanism for parents to use these services by displacing any concerns they may have about the negative consequences of using them. Demonstrating that there are rigorous checks in place to ensure the highest quality of provision furthers that persuasive agenda and can be seen articulated very clearly in the introduction of inspection regimes (considered further on p. 29). Yet the quality of provision can be in tension with a desire to ensure affordability and we often see this within national policy as governments look to adjust quality requirements in an attempt to make services more affordable.

Further tensions in the dual strands of early years policy are discussed by Moss (2006) in regard to the structure and purpose of early years services. There is a history of some countries developing one set of services to meet the needs of working parents and another set to begin the education journey of young children. In some instances, this has resulted in services being fragmented. This fragmentation not only relates to the purpose of the services, but also other aspects such as funding and qualification requirements. Many countries (including the UK) have now embarked on a journey of aiming to integrate these services. In fact, the OECD advocates the adoption of integrated approaches (Neuman, 2005) and uses the term early childhood education and care (ECEC) to represent how it sees educating and caring for children as being inseparable in understandings and constructions of early years services. As such, care and education are co-located both in relation to the physical provision of services and the philosophical thinking behind services. Mahon and McBride (2009) discuss how the OECD acts as a powerful purveyor of knowledge. Reviews such as the four Starting Strong reports synthesise what is happening in early years services around the world and disseminate knowledge on what they identify as good practice. The construction of knowledge is important as it creates a set of truths around best practice (something that we will return to later). What Mahon and McBride raise is the powerful force of supranational organisations in shaping policy agendas. The degree of influence will obviously vary according to the findings of the particular report, but in the UK Stating Strong has had a formidable influence.

In the UK, the National Childcare Strategy, first introduced in 1998 under the Green Paper Meeting the Childcare Challenge (DfEE, 1998), has seen moves towards creating a more integrated approach. The Green Paper repeatedly refers to 'integrated early education and childcare' services. At times, **'educare'** has been used as shorthand to represent the notion that early years services are about both education and care. Since 1998, there have been various initiatives to continue the work of integrating care and education: early years and childcare services now being the responsibility of the same Ministry (the Department for Education); the creation of one inspection framework where previously there had been separate care and education inspection regimes; and the development of a single curriculum: the Early Years Foundation Stage (EYFS). These developments in early years policy in England (with other parts of the UK adopting similar patterns, see Selbie et al., 2015 and Wincott, 2004) represent how there have been a number of structural changes to formulate a more integrated approach. However, changes in some structural features only seek to highlight where there are still differences, such as early years education being a free entitlement and childcare being subsidised. Policy developments in the UK have suggested that care and education have not always been regarded as equal in the emphasis of policy. In 2013, concerns were raised that the More Great Childcare document (DfE, 2013), published under the Conservative–Liberal Democrat coalition, privileged affordability and availability over quality, training and experience (Calder et al., 2013; Neville, 2013; Ransom, 2013). Whilst early years policy looks to present a focus (albeit with a different emphasis) on care and education, we have to ask whether it is possible to have this dual focus and what it means for the delivery of services. The dual focus of early years policy will take on different meanings for each of the stakeholders and even then there will be variation in interpretations, as we discuss in the next chapter – importantly, as a leader, do you see yourself as leading a care service, an education service or an educare service?

European Interests

The European Union (EU) represents another example of an organisation that has acknowledged the dual role of early years services. Initially focused on economic co-operation, the EU is now concerned with the socio-economics of member states. The EU takes on a slightly different role to the OECD as it is able to create law and treaties that individual countries are expected to ratify (or in some cases are able to opt out of). Again, the EU has been influential in terms of early years policy. Where once it focused on the quantity of places (due to its role in supporting parental employment), it is now increasingly focused on the quality of provision (Campbell-Barr and Nygård, 2014). Arguably, the shift of focus represents a progression in how early years services are framed, the former quantitative exercise being about parental employment, the latter more focused on child development. The shift in emphasis could be taken as evidence that early years policy in the EU (and the UK) may still be evolving. However, whilst the EU has a role in shaping national policy its influence only extends so far, as is evident in differences in how individual countries structure and fund early years services. These differences will be a result of the many different views on the relevance of quality early years provision in different countries.

Why the Interest in Quality Early Years Services?

The investment by national governments into early years services represents a **social investment** strategy. Social investment represents the economic monies spent by governments (and charitable organisations in some instances) to achieve predetermined economic and social goals. We have already outlined the dual aims of early years policy and to some extent they represent the economic and social goals that governments are looking to achieve. Yet we return to the idea of why *quality* early years services and not just early years services. To focus on just the provision of services as a quantitative exercise to increase the number of places available would support the objectives around parental employment, as can be identified in EU policy making historically. However, there is now a clear focus from the EU and other supranational organisations on quality. This focus on quality represents a social investment strategy that is interested in the economic and social advantages that investing in the early years can offer.

The evidence base for the social advantages of quality early years provision draws on psychology-based studies. Psychology has provided a way to understand child development, classifying and normalising what is to be expected of a child (Dahlberg and Moss, 2005). Initial studies focused on the potential negative impacts of non-maternal care (Fenech, 2011). Historical constructions of maternal care as the best form of care, largely drawing on attachment theories, started to look out of date as mothers began to combine work and family life. Research studies began to consider whether time in childcare could have any negative consequences for children. Studies such as that of the National Institute of Child Health and Human Development (NICHD) explored child development in relation to the hours spent in care. The NICHD study is important as it started the process of establishing that it was not just the time spent in care that was important, but also the quality of care provided. Over time, research studies considering the benefits of early years services were undertaken and evaluated (Fenech, 2011). The research has now developed to a stage where quality early years services are accepted, without question, as offering a sound social investment in child development.

The social advantages interplay with economic ones to create an understanding whereby early years provision is seen as being good socially, it supports children's development, but this is also good economically. The economic advantages of having more people in work and paying taxes can be accepted when considering the relationship to maternal employment that we discussed earlier, but the economic advantages of investing in children need a bit more consideration. Investing in early years services is regarded as an investment in the future, whereby children who do well developmentally will grow up to be successful adults who are less likely to be dependent on the state. In particular, the socio-economic perspective of early years services represents an equality driver, whereby those from disadvantaged backgrounds have the most to gain from good quality early years services, both in relation to their development and in terms of reduced economic spending on them in the future – something widely advocated by both the OECD and the EU.

The socio-economic perspective of early years services can be understood in relation to **human capital theory**. Human capital theory has become a persuasive economic argument for investing in early years services. Framed by notions of a global knowledge economy, investing in one's knowledge and skills is seen to be advantageous at the individual level as those with the most knowledge will arguably get higher economic returns when they enter the labour market, but equally, at a country level, having a knowledgeable workforce will better position a country to compete in global markets in the future. Early developments of human capital theory did not discuss early years services, but more recently economists have increasingly advocated an investment in early years as an investment in the foundations of an individual's lifelong learning (Campbell-Barr, 2012). The economist and Nobel Prize winner James Heckman has played a key role in promoting the socio-economic advantages of early years provision. Heckman's work has indicated that there is more to gain from investments in early years services than from investments in any other stage of education, at any other point in the life course. On the one hand an investment in the young has more to gain as it has more time in which to grow to fruition, but on the other, it is also that 'learning begets learning and skills acquired early on make later learning easier' (Heckman, 2000: 4). Framed in relation to lifelong learning agendas, early years provision is thus seen to create the foundations for later learning.

However, Heckman has cautioned policy makers in the interpretations that they make when formulating an understanding of value from early years services. Investments in early years services should reflect an investment in all forms of knowledge, but the concern is that what is increasingly being valued are cognitive skills, and other skills become hidden or not considered important (see Heckman, 2000). When looking at definitions of human capital theory from supranational organisations, it is evident that they identify with notions of a broad range of knowledge and skills, but the extent to which this translates into national policy is questionable:

> Human capital is defined by the OECD as the knowledge, skills, competencies and attributes embodied in individuals that facilitate the creation of personal, social and economic well-being. (Keely, 2008: 29)

> Human Capital, understood broadly in terms of skills, both cognitive and noncognitive, as well as capabilities, such as health or social functioning, is one of the foremost determinants of welfare. (Freidman and Sturdy, 2011: 51)

It is important to recognise that investments in human capital are framed by understandings of a global knowledge economy, whereby knowledge is regarded as key to economic competitiveness. The economic focus on human capital means that there is an interest in the economic savings that can be made for both the individual and society through investing in early years services. Influential studies on human capital and early years provision include the Perry Preschool Programme (High Scope), the Abecedarian and the Chicago Child Parent Centres. Famously, they have created a perception that for every one dollar invested, seven can be saved (Campbell-Barr, 2012). However, they have been criticised due to their small sample sizes, for the early years interventions being targeted at specific sections of the population rather than being universal, and with the studies based in America there are questions as to their applicability in other contexts (Campbell-Barr, 2012; Penn, 2010).

More recently, the UK has developed a longitudinal research project on the benefits of early years services: the Effective Provision of Pre-school Education (EPPE) project. Following more than 3000 children from the age of 3 years, it has tracked their developmental and academic attainment. The project considered children's attendance (and non-attendance) at various pre-school environments to explore associations between features of practice and child outcomes. In 2014, findings were published on the GCSE results of those in the study, demonstrating lasting effects of quality pre-school on maths and English grades (Sammons et al., 2014). Whilst a value-for-money assessment was not an original objective of the study, a sub-study (Catton et al., 2014) conducted an economic analysis of the savings that could be made to the Exchequer. The economic analysis estimated that there was a benefit of around £26,000 for individuals and £36,000 for households, resulting in a benefit of approximately £16,000 per household for the Exchequer. When comparing high and low levels of quality, a difference of around £12,000 for individuals was identified (Sylva et al., 2014: 19–20). The economic benefits are based on GCSE performance and predicted individual incomes, so the authors (Catton et al., 2014) do note caution in interpreting the findings.

Hegemonic Views of Early Years Services

We do not question the notion that quality early years services offer value, but what we would query is how that sense of value is determined. Whilst we welcome the investment in early years services by governments and the support from supranational organisations to focus on the quality of provision, we have concerns around the hegemonic view of early years services in terms of the assumptions of quality and effective leadership that underpin the activity. What the examples of the OECD and the EU represent is not only a global interest in the quality of early years services, but also the concept of a set of shared understandings around early years services and how they might be led. A hegemonic approach (whereby there is one global view of early years services) neglects to consider the local in the provision of early years services. By the local we are not just thinking about national governments, rather we are also thinking about the process by which national governments interpret global views on early years services and how these are then disseminated to and implemented by local practitioners. In other words, what does all of the above mean for a nursery in a city such as Plymouth or a rural location such as Dartmoor?

Whilst there is a filtering process whereby national governments will make sense of supranational ideas and local practitioners will make sense of national policy, it is worth reflecting on the privileging of developed (western) countries' perspectives. As Dahlberg and Moss (2005) consider, it is Anglo-American ideas that are heard across the world, whilst Penn (2010) refers to the Global South and Carter Dillon (2013) to the Eurocentric. The concern is that whilst there is a global interest in early years services, the knowledge production around quality is not shaped equally by all areas of the world. Often, those countries that are still developing their early years provision are encouraged to adopt approaches that have been demonstrated to 'work' in other countries. However, if we take the example of early years services providing the foundations for lifelong learning in regard to human capital theory, is the knowledge that is required in the UK going to be the same as that required in a country such as the Gambia? Carter Dillon (2013) talks of observing an early years class in the Gambia where children were learning phonics underpinned by English approaches, including using references such as T-T-T-Tennis that may not be culturally appropriate. Penn (2010) also discusses the cultural sensitivities of organisations, such as the World Bank developing a human capital calculator for countries to predict the rate of return of investing in the early years. Where is there a consideration of things such as race and class or other inequalities such as child mortality?

De Sousa Santos is a sociology professor who has questioned the influence of supranational organisations and whether there is in fact a need to think about globalisation in the plural (globalisations) in order to recognise that one global view might be misplaced. It is not just that the supranational can be misplaced in the local, but also that it is likely that it is the local context that will give rise to the solutions needed as a society (Dalea and Robertson, 2004). Applying this to human capital perspectives of early years services questions the relevance (or even the possibility) of having a one-size-fits-all approach, as seems to be evident in the thinking of supranational organisations. Consider this just in regard to men and women, particularly in countries where gender equality is underdeveloped: will men and women require the same skill set to secure their future economic success? Further, there is the question of what the influence of supranational organisations hides, of what is not seen and acknowledged in approaches to early years services.

We feel that the influence of supranational organisations has been important for raising the profile of early years services. However, rather than seeking a hegemonic approach to quality and the leading of that quality in early years services, we believe that there is strength to be drawn in the differences that occur between countries and even early years providers within countries. Global discussions are good as they open up alternative ways of looking at things (Dahlberg and Moss, 2005) and allow us to see other possibilities. As Penn (2011b) has argued, international perspectives can limit parochialism and help to ascertain why it is that there is a particular approach or understanding. The process of looking at something different is what helps to develop our own practice, whether that is in terms of national policy or in individual settings; without difference we may become complacent with our own parochialism and thereby run the risk of becoming irrelevant and out of touch very quickly.

Cultural Interpretations of Early Years Services

In recognition of the importance of global variations, it is evident that definitions of quality early years services need to reflect cultural values around the intended goals for investing in early years services (often developmental) of different countries (Rosenthal, 2003). National quality assessment tools are often about assessing quality with regards to the desired, culturally determined goals and expectations of early years services (Moyles et al., 2002). Thus, whilst supranational organisations will seek to offer advice and guidance on early years policy, that advice and guidance will interplay with cultural values and socio-political philosophies. Some of the features will be shaped by socio-cultural views on children, childhood and families. For example, the change in understandings of women's role, whereby increasingly women combine paid employment with family life in many countries, has informed a shift in views around early years services (albeit that policy often still assumes nuclear families headed by a male). Cultural understandings also interplay with the socio-economics of a country – are there sufficient funds to invest in early years services? Are there particular economic difficulties (such as child poverty or serious national deficit) that a country is looking to address? All of these considerations will interact with the history of a country and events that have taken place. There are therefore a number of interweaving factors that will combine to create a common set of desirable outcomes and these outcomes will shape understandings of quality (Penn, 2011b). Each country will therefore have a set of ideas about the role of early years services, albeit one that will have a global turn.

The social, economic, political and cultural features of a country will also interplay with theoretical developments. As Rosenthal (2003) has outlined, often understandings of goals and outcomes in the early years are shaped by ideas of child development and developmentally appropriate practice. Psychological theories of child development have been influential in shaping not only understandings of children and childhood, but also the services that are provided for them. The influence of child development theories within the equality agendas that have been outlined in relation to the social investment justification for investing in early years services put forward by supranational organisations is evident. There is an underpinning philosophy that all children should be at a predetermined stage at any one point in their lives (Rosenthal, 2003). Poverty and social disadvantage are thus regarded as problematic as some children have not reached the culturally prescribed stages and need additional support to bring them into line with their peers. Investment in early years services therefore becomes about investing in children in order to limit differences in children's development, irrespective of their socio-economic status, thereby creating a stable forward trajectory that can be used for economic planning.

Regarding early years as a social investment strategy says a lot about how a society values its children. Under human capital theory, children are valued on the basis of what they will become – educated and economically active adults. Childhood therefore becomes a path to adulthood rather than an important stage in its own right. There are also implications for practice as quality practice is shaped by what it takes for a child to do well and how to get them there. In England, doing well is defined as being ready to take on the challenges of school and to achieve high academic success and this is clearly seen in the debates on school readiness. Numerous studies have explored how practitioners feel burdened by top-down bureaucratic expectations of measuring and assessing children's development (Adams et al., 2004; Coleyshaw et al., 2012; Cottle and Alexander, 2012). So if practitioners feel pressured over expectations around child development and policy makers do not recognise the importance of childhood as a current state rather than just a path to adulthood, why assess children's development? The appeal of developmental stages is that there is a sense that they can be reduced to a set of pre-determined criteria – a set of measures. These measures can be used to assess the quality of provision in relation to the desired outcomes. Measures are important as they are seen as a set of objective and reliable features that can be assessed in order to determine both outcomes and quality, but this is not to say that they are not problematic.

Modernist Approaches to Quality

Modernity reflects a period in history, but also a way of thinking that emerged at the time and which has had a lasting legacy (Dahlberg et al., 2013). Although there are disputes as to when modernity started – the sixteenth, seventeenth or eighteenth century (Dahlberg and Moss, 2005) – modernity reflects the privileging of a rational, objective, empirical (scientific) view of the world. The focus is on creating a knowable world, grounded in scientific evidence. Bernstein (1996) discusses the development of statistics in history; statistics enabled the ability to count those who do not fit the norm and to look at ways of 'fixing' them.

Within Anglo-American cultures, understandings of appropriate stages of development are shaped by middle-class norms as to 'normal' development (see Rosenthal, 2003). In the case of early years provision, children are assessed against normal rates of child development and the fixing becomes about looking at quality in relation to settings that can achieve the desired outcomes. But then it becomes a self-fulfilling prophecy – as particular features are identified as being good for child development, there are attempts to reinforce them. Developmental norms become about prescription, rather than description (Dahlberg and Moss, 2005). If X will lead to Y, more evidence is collated to support this rather than to stop and question the evidence. For example, the qualifications of those working in the early years will have an influence on the quality of provision, but if you stop to think about this in more detail, what is it about the qualifications that makes the difference – writing essays, learning about theory, reflecting on practice or being dedicated to study?

In favouring scientific rationality, assessments of quality become a quantitative exercise, whereby quality and child outcomes are reduced to a set of measures in order to consider any correlations. Early years provision becomes a site for producing predetermined (educational) outcomes through the application of technical practices (Dahlberg and Moss, 2005). Quantitative approaches are favoured as they are regarded as objective and reliable (Campbell-Barr et al., 2011). In particular, if we return to the studies that informed human capital perspectives on early years services (pp. 17–18), we can see how they are symbolic of what is often regarded as the gold standard of research. They are quantitative and use randomised controlled trials (Hodkinson, 2004). Such approaches are upheld in research as being both rigorous and reliable. The data provides a view of 'what works' in policy making (Ball, 2008).

Mathers et al. (2012) suggest that assessments of quality can be understood in relation to process and **structural quality**, whilst also acknowledging that these have a relationship to child outcomes. **Process quality** is about the child's experience (e.g. interactions with staff), whilst structural quality is about features such as group size and ratios. The former is accepted as being harder to assess than the latter as it requires in-depth observation and skilled analysis that looks widely rather than narrowly at the evidence. In a modernist world, observations are reduced to measureable indicators that are simpler to apply and offer comparative study and the opportunity to chart progression. Mathers et al. (2012) discuss the Early Childhood Environment Rating Scale (ECERS), which is a global quality assessment tool that is widely used in research. Trained observers assess quality by considering a series of aspects about the early years practice being observed. Each aspect has a seven-point scale with a statement against each point. If the observer agrees with the first statement, they move on to the next; if they agree again, they move on until they reach a point where they feel they cannot move up the scale any further, thus providing the score. These scores can then be used to look for relationships with child outcomes, for example.

One difficulty with the modernist approach is that it can start to hide the original problem. Society is looking to combat social inequalities to improve the life chances of children, but this means that children have become a project to get 'right'. Children reflect wider social problems with childhood being the period of time when society needs to get things 'right' (Dahlberg and Moss, 2005). Modernist approaches or quantifiable indicators not only enable society to identify those children who need additional support, they also allow us to track whether the support is working. Practice becomes technocratic as practitioners internalise knowledge of quality and enact what they believe is good for children (Urban, 2008), partly because research is reduced to measures and assessment and this is what guides practice, but also because power dynamics privilege the knowledge that reflects the 'right' outcomes.

Through the construction of an evidence base, a series of discourses are formed that shape understandings of quality. Discourses represent a way of viewing, thinking and speaking about the social world and seek to normalise behaviour (Dahlberg et al., 2013). Discourses conceal assumptions and render political objectives and ideologies invisible as dominant ideas become the taken-for-granted way of thinking (Dahlberg and Moss, 2005). For example, quality is often considered in relation to staffing, the involvement of parents, group size, interactions, the nature of the premises, health and safety, the curriculum and so on as these are often features in both research and quality assessments (see Melhuish, 2004). However, consider these features of quality as a discursive construction and questions arise as to why these features have been privileged over others. Is it just that such features uphold the desired (normative) way of thinking about the world? In considering understandings of quality in relation to discourse, it highlights that there is a power dynamic in the process of which discourses become dominant over others, thereby privileging some knowledge over other knowledge. Policy makers will privilege particular ways of thinking about the world and can use research to support their ideologies (Urban, 2008). Modernist approaches come with their own cultural values and principles. Through considering them as discursive constructs, it is possible to analyse how they reflect what it is that a particular culture has constructed as being important. If we return to the example of ECERS, the revised version of the scale (ECERS-R) was used by Sylva et al. (2004) in the EPPE study. The scale was supplemented during the course of the longitudinal project by the development of ECERS-E (Sylva et al., 2010) to encompass additional assessments for Literacy, Maths, Science and Environments and Diversity. In incorporating these assessments and in considering the recent value-for-money assessments that we discussed earlier, it tells us a great deal about the cultural values around what are deemed to be important features of early years practice.

Modernist approaches to assessing quality help to inform our understandings of quality, but it is important to be aware of what is falling between the gaps of the measurements (what detail might be missing) and who it is that determines what is measured. If we return to the idea of hegemonic ways of thinking about early years services, we can in fact see that there are some collective assumptions about children and child development that are guiding the development of services. They are presented as a series of truths – for example, if quality early years services are provided, children will go on to be successful adults. Whilst we do not dispute the positive differences that early years services can make in children's lives, we would like to suggest that human capital theory and research such as EPPE is just one way of thinking about quality.

Post-structuralist Approaches to Quality

Post-structuralism allows us to question the supposed certainty and objectivity that have been presented by modern approaches. Post-structuralism is often used interchangeably with post-modernism, but post-modernism tends to be used as an umbrella term for a number of theories that developed in response to a dissatisfaction with modernist approaches. Our focus on post-structuralism is intentional as it emphasises the notion of deconstructing the supposed certainty of the knowledge that is presented to us. Post-structuralist approaches challenge the construction that there is absolute knowledge (Pound, 2011) – it deconstructs what is believed to be a given reality, asking questions of knowledge and commonly held truths in order to problematise how (in this instance) quality has been constructed. If you view modernity as a series of building blocks that enable us to build up quality early years provision, post-structuralism is the idea that there is more than one way to connect the building blocks. As a leader, you are able to take different building blocks and use them to construct a version of quality that is meaningful to your context. You might have particular features that you want to use to create a firm foundation on which to place your other building blocks or you might feel that your building blocks change their construction for each group of children that you work with. Post-structuralism encourages you to think not only about how you want to construct your building blocks, but also to think about why.

If we return to the idea of discourse, post-structuralist approaches enable us to deconstruct the supposed truth of the dominant ways of thinking about early years practice. We have already considered that there is a power dynamic involved in the discursive production of quality. In investing in early years services, governments will work hard to secure their investment and construct a correct way of thinking about early years provision (Osgood, 2006). As MacNaughton (2005) has outlined, there are some deeply ingrained ways of thinking about early years practice and their familiarity can make them feel right. For example, in Chapter 5 we explore some of the ways early years services are described, such as 'child centred', and suggest that the common use of such terminology means that there is often no attempt to think about where the terminology has come from or what it really means. Post-structuralist approaches ask us to be aware of the power dynamics involved in constructing such terminology, but also to deconstruct them. As outlined at the start of this chapter, quality is frequently used as a prefix to early years, but rarely is there a consideration of what has shaped and informed understandings of quality. In taking apart the building blocks, it is possible to consider what has fallen between the gaps of the discursive production of early years services, but also how it is that they have been put together.

Reflection Point

Consider why it is that you feel early years services are important. Is it about care, education or educare? Can you identify where these ideas have come from: who or what has shaped them? Do you identify with the policy objectives of supranational organisations or national governments, or is there something about your local context that you feel is important?

In the next chapter, we continue to look at the construction of discursive truths around the quality of early years services, but we do so critically. Building on the idea of post-modernism, we will present some of the cracks that are present in understandings of quality, whilst also looking at how research on practitioners, parents and children can provide us with alternative ways of thinking about quality in the early years.

Chapter Summary

- Quality early years provision is a global issue.
- Quality early years provision supports parental employment and child development.
- Understandings of quality are shaped by how the purpose of early years services is constructed.
- Understandings of the purpose of early years services have been shaped by child development and human capital theories that are largely derived from the developed world.
- Quality needs to account for the local.
- Post-structuralism asks who has constructed the knowledge on quality early years services and why.

Further Reading

Heckman, J. (2000) *Invest in the Very Young*. Chicago, IL: Ounce of Prevention Fund and the University of Chicago Harris School of Public Policy Studies. Available at: www.montanakidscount.com/fileaccess/getfile/20.pdf (accessed 15 October 2015)

This is a short paper that provides an overview of the economic debates around the provision of early years services.

Urban, M. (2008) 'Dealing with uncertainty: challenges and possibilities for the early childhood profession', *European Early Childhood Education Research Journal*, 16 (2): 135–52.

This article explores much of what we have outlined in this chapter regarding dominant discourses and how they become ingrained in understandings of early years services, particularly in regard to what it means to be a professional working in the early years. This reading is therefore helpful in developing your thinking for this and later chapters.

WHAT IS QUALITY? EXPLORING THE EVIDENCE BASE

2

Chapter Overview

In the previous chapter, we considered the reasons for investing in early years provision and how these impact on the way quality is defined. Whilst there is a favouring of measuring quality due to the supposed objectivity of such approaches and the ability to look for correlations between sets of measures, we feel that quality is far more complex than this. In this chapter, we look at research that highlights how complex it is to define quality early years services. We explore research that presents us with alternative views on quality to those we explored in the previous chapter. We highlight the contradictions between different pieces of research and embrace them. Recognising that there are different views of quality allows for a meaning of quality that is right for the children that you work with. We begin by considering the role of external surveillance systems (quality inspections) as a form of technocratic control in regard to the discursive truths of quality before moving on to consider that they present just one way of thinking about quality. We then move on to discuss the views of practitioners, parents and children and how their perspectives challenge modernist views of quality.

Quality Frameworks

Many countries will have systems in place for monitoring the quality of early years provision, but the reasons for monitoring can vary in their scope, purpose and application. In some countries, such as Germany and

Hungary, local regions monitor early years providers (i.e. kindergartens), whilst in others there will be a national approach. The UK sits somewhere between these two as each of the four countries that form the UK (England, Scotland, Ireland and Wales) have their own system for inspecting and monitoring provision. The inspection process in the UK is important not only as it acts as a guide for what is regarded as quality (and the related outcomes), but also as it acts as a trigger for being able to draw down government funding, such as that for the allocation of the free early years education places or, in the case of tax credits, parents can only claim them when using a registered provider.

If we focus on the example of England, we can consider in more detail how the registration process has evolved and how it functions. The process in England was originally under a local authority inspection and regulation system, whereby each local authority inspected the early years providers in its area. Historically, key legislation such as the Nurseries and Child-Minders Regulations Act of 1948, and its subsequent revision in 1968, focused mainly on the appropriateness of the setting, the health of staff members and the adherence to very practical standards such as ratios of staff to children and the amount of space that should be provided. Thus, expectations about quality of a setting were minimal, with leadership being far from an integral aspect of the registration and inspection process. Quality, as understood by historic registration processes, saw the management of the setting as more important than leadership with a focus on keeping and maintaining basic records; claiming government grants and subsidies, as well as collecting fees and paying bills. Over time, governments have scrutinised the inspection process (and continue to do so). A significant change for early years came about in 2004 when the Office for Standards in Education, Children's Services and Skills (Ofsted) was introduced to inspect all early years providers, creating a national system with significantly more expectations of similarity and coherence than was previously the case. Prior to taking on the inspection of early years providers, Ofsted was already inspecting schools, but its remit has grown as indicated by its full title. In the early days, there was criticism that Ofsted's training and expertise were in school education rather than in early years provision, leading to anxiety that its findings, assessments and recommendations would be fundamentally flawed. Concerns over the knowledge of inspectors were also raised when inspections were contracted out to external agencies, although such practices are becoming less common. Initially, under the Ofsted inspection there were separate care and education inspections in the early years relating to either the care of the children or the educational aspects of a setting, resulting in some providers being inspected twice, and there were significant variations in requirements for the different sectors. However, this has all changed and there is now one single inspection framework for all early years providers. In England, the inspection system grades providers using a scale of: Outstanding, Good, Requires Improvement or Inadequate. There is evidence suggesting that both the grades and the reports produced by Ofsted are hard to understand for parents (Mathers et al., 2012) and evidence that practitioners can find it hard to understand the inspection framework (see Callender, 2000; Gilroy and Wilcox, 1997). However, the data around school and practitioner understandings of Ofsted requirements are dated now, suggesting that providers may have become more adept at interpreting the requirements.

Inspection and monitoring systems via national and local governments are often criticised as they present quality early years provision as fixed and objective (Tanner et al., 2006). Curriculums and quality frameworks represent an official definition of quality that is tied to a set of desirable outcomes (as we explored in the last chapter). Ebbeck and Waniganayake (2003) discuss how government standards and rules reflect that government's interests and what it sees as important. One criticism of this approach is that quality becomes a static entity. It can be static if governments do not look to regularly review their quality criteria, but it can also be static if a provider believes that it has achieved the desired quality criteria and this limits them in exploring alternative perspectives. Research into the perspectives of local authorities in England has found that this can happen, whereby early years providers who do well in their inspections believe they are 'untouchable' and no longer need to look to develop their practice (Campbell-Barr, 2009b; Mathers et al., 2012). A second criticism relates to how the assessment is undertaken. Any assessment of quality, whether it is a rating scale such as ECERS (Fenech, 2011) or an inspection via Ofsted, is merely a snapshot in time. For practitioners, this can feel very frustrating – why did Ofsted have to turn up on a day when the room leader was ill? The argument against this is that any setting should be able to ensure quality no matter what has happened on a given day. There are also concerns around how frequently the inspections take place. In England, under Ofsted, inspections should take place every three years, but this can vary if a specific concern is raised or the manager changes. Whilst these instances can trigger an early inspection, it is possible for inspections to be delayed if a provider achieved an outstanding grade on its last inspection.

There are also criticisms as to the difference that the inspection process can make to the quality of provision. The data pertaining to the early years sector is limited, but evidence from schools suggests that the usefulness of an inspection can be dependent on the qualities of the inspector and their relationship with the leader of the setting, such as how the results are communicated (Ehren and Visscher, 2006). Matthews and Sammons (2004) explore Ofsted's claim of 'improvement through inspection' and suggest that there is no connection between inspection and improvement.

Rosenthal (2004), looking at secondary schools, similarly found that following an inspection, there was no positive impact on the exam results of the school. Hopkins et al. (2010) looked for correlations between Ofsted scores and children's Early Years Foundation Stage (EYFS) profile data and found that an Ofsted score was not a predictor of EYFS results. However, it is important to remember when looking at headline findings such as these that there are a number of variables that can interplay. Attending an outstanding early years provider (or school) does not automatically result in high outcomes for children, due to the impact of the socio-economics of a child's family (for example). Equally, whilst a setting may not do well in its Ofsted inspection, this is not to say that it is meeting the needs of the community in which it is located (something we return to in Chapter 4).

It is important to recognise that different measures will have different objectives. For example, an Ofsted inspection is not designed to be a comprehensive detailed examination of quality, rather its purpose is the monitoring of early years provision. However, whilst Ofsted may not provide a comprehensive measure of quality, even ECERS, which is designed to be thorough, does not cover all details and it is often the intangible that is missing (Fenech, 2011). Mathers et al. (2012) explored the relationship between Ofsted grades and ECERS-R and ECERS-E grades. In addition, they looked at the relationship between Ofsted grades and the Infant and Toddler Environment Rating Scale (ITERS), which measures the quality of care for children from birth to 2.5 years (whilst ECERS goes from 2.5 to 5). Mathers et al. emphasise that these rating scales have a different objective to Ofsted in terms of the detail that they are looking at when assessing quality, so some differences could be anticipated. Interestingly, the findings indicate that quality, as assessed by Ofsted, looks to be broadly in line with what is being assessed by ECERS, but when looking at ITERS there is no correlation. The suggestion is that understandings of quality in England have been shaped by needs and policy objectives around 3- and 4-year-olds. In some respects, this is not surprising as initial policy interventions in England were focused on expanding the amount and improving the quality of early years places for 3- and 4-year-olds, but since 2014 early years education provision has been provided to disadvantaged 2-year-olds, raising questions as to whether there are differences in what quality means for 2-year-olds when compared to 3- and 4-year-olds.

Research by Georgeson et al. (2014) has looked in more detail at understandings of quality for 2-year-olds. The research involved exploring what policy stakeholders (at national and local levels), leaders and practitioners felt constituted quality early years provision for 2-year-olds. Whilst the project was focused on 2-year-olds, one of the key findings was that participants in the research felt that quality was a complete package and not one that was fragmented by the age of the child. Participants made the point that they would adjust activities and resources in regard to the needs of the child, but felt that age was not the only variable. In other words, quality for 3- and 4-year-olds is a part of quality for 2-year-olds. However, what the research of Georgeson et al. also highlights is that quality is more than just a rating scale or what is captured in an Ofsted inspection; some participants in the research raised concerns over the reliability of Ofsted inspections for the reasons given above. In recognising that quality was more than a rating scale, it became apparent to the researchers that it was a complex and multifaceted term.

Quality Outside the Rating Scales Box

The difficulty with modernist approaches to quality is that they are shaped by a set of predetermined, measureable indicators. Within these measures of quality, what cannot be measured is lost. Fenech (2011) explores how understandings of quality cannot capture the intangible, such as morality and spirituality. Other research also points to aspects of quality that practitioners, parents and children identify as important, but that do not feature in formal assessments of quality. For example, returning to Georgeson et al.'s (2014) research, staffing was recognised as being central to quality, and whilst many of the respondents spoke about qualifications, there was also discussion of a set of skills that sit alongside formal qualification structures – those that might be regard as dispositions, such as being caring and empathetic. Cottle and Alexander (2012) also explore how early years practitioners discuss their role in slippery terms using the idea of a feel and an ethos. Thus, whilst practitioners respond to the quality agendas as set out by Ofsted, they also have an ethics of care that guides their practice (Osgood, 2006, 2012).

Moyles (2001) has discussed how there is a paradox between the heart and professionalism. As Campbell-Barr (2014) has outlined, policy discourses surrounding the provision of early years services have looked to create an entrepreneurial discourse, whereby providers are businesslike and professional. Such discursive productions of early years provision have been a mechanism to try and mould the character of early years provision so that it is sustainable (therefore a wise investment for policy makers) and productive. The entrepreneurial discourse complements the managerialist discourse that is imposed through inspection and monitoring processes (Campbell-Barr, 2014). As we will discuss in more detail in Chapter 3, such understandings of early years services have consequences for those who are leading them as they presuppose that leadership is an entrepreneurial act informed by managerialist models, thus privileging outcomes over process and leaving little room for the relational aspects of the setting. Such technocratic understandings of early years provision have been at odds with those within the sector who construct their understandings of the role in relation to love and an ethic of care (Moyles, 2001). McGillivray (2008) discusses how the historical roots of early years provision lie within a desire to nurture and protect children, and Osgood (2004, 2006) explores how such constructions of early years provision sit uneasily with the more entrepreneurial and managerialist discourses that are proposed by policy makers.

In their research with early years practitioners, Cottle and Alexander (2012) acknowledge that it is often about playing two games – one is meeting the needs of Ofsted, the other is responding to beliefs about how best to work with children. However, Cottle and Alexander add that the beliefs of a practitioner do not always match their actions, giving rise to an uncomfortable dissonance that has to be managed by the individual. There has been a recent rise in research looking at early years provision within reception classes and exploring how teachers are feeling increasingly constrained by the datafication of their practice (Roberts-Holmes, 2014). Pressures to ensure that children are reaching expected levels of attainment is resulting in some practitioners feeling that they are not able to adopt the child-led, play-based approach advocated in the EYFS in the way that they would like. Such research highlights how often our values and beliefs around what leaders and practitioners would like to be doing and what they think they should be doing can be compromised by policy objectives. In Chapter 4, we examine the toxic effects of this compromise, leading us to suggest that policy efforts to improve the leadership of quality may have the opposite result, with good leaders leaving the sector, unable to cope any longer with the dissonance between what they believe and what they are being asked to do.

The experience of providers highlights how there is a mismatch between what policy makers think and what practitioners think. One of the key issues is who it is that determines the quality structures. The above evidence shows how the voice of the practitioner is not heard within policy-making arenas. There is some evidence to suggest that policy listens to research, as we would suggest that the correlation between ECERS and Ofsted in the Mathers et al. (2012) study is the result of the use of ECERS in studies such as EPPE. The outcome is that there is a reflection of ECERS in the Ofsted requirements as policy has looked to put into practice the findings of the EPPE study (see Chapter 1). However, the lack of an association between the views of early years practitioners and official views of quality does not feel right to us. Why develop a system that does not reflect the views of the people who surely best understand the system – the early years practitioners? There are two answers here that we would like to explore.

The first, the desire to demonstrate 'what works' (as discussed in Chapter 1), focuses on assessing the difference that early years provision can make for children, families and wider society, which fits a model whereby we can measure the difference. This means that things such as love, compassion, emotion and patience, those aspects that are not measurable constructs, are left out of official understandings of quality early years provision. And, to be honest, would you want an Ofsted inspector assessing whether or not you love a child? The second reason why the practitioner's voice is absent in policy making is related to the idea of accountability. As we discussed in the introduction, the early years model in England (and other parts of the UK) is reliant on a mixed market of providers, whereby the private, voluntary, independent and maintained sectors are all involved in providing services. In fact, much of early years provision in England is reliant on the private sector (Lloyd and Penn, 2010). This creates something of a conundrum for policy makers. How can they ensure that private sector providers will work to fulfil policy objectives? The introduction of an external surveillance system, such as Ofsted, enables policy makers to monitor early years providers in fulfilling policy objectives and make demands relating to training and systemic changes. This monitoring is about whether providers are adhering to the guidance that has been set out, but another way of framing it is whether providers are adhering to the policy objectives that have been set out by government. Are early years providers putting in place the things that are needed to achieve the desired child outcomes? In viewing inspection and monitoring processes as being about adhering to policy, it is evident how they are embedded in a system of accountability (Case et al., 2000).

The Panoptic Gaze

Post-modernism tends to be used as an umbrella term to refer to a number of different theoretical ways of thinking that arose out of dissatisfaction with modernism (as we outlined in Chapter 1), but we are specifically focusing on post-structuralist approaches as they look to challenge the notion of the rational and coherent knowledge that is present in modernist approaches (MacNaughton, 2005). The French philosopher Foucault was interested in developing a critique of modernist perspectives and he did this by considering the interplay between power and knowledge within society. In drawing on the ideas of Foucault, we can consider the power dynamics involved in the regulation of quality in the early years and how certain attributes become taken-for-granted features of quality early years provision.

We have already considered in this chapter that a system of accountability is important in a mixed-market model of early years provision as it enables the monitoring of provision. However, it is much deeper than just monitoring what providers do. In the last chapter, we outlined why it is that governments are interested in early years provision. Increasingly, the interest is being framed in relation to human capital agendas, whereby the early years provide the foundation for all later stages of development. Whether the policy interest in early years services is framed in relation to forming the foundations for later learning, supporting child development or something else that we have not considered in our discussion, the outcome is the same. Policy makers want to monitor provision to ensure that it is going to lead to the outcomes they have identified as desirable. This requires a degree of standardisation, predictability and control (Dahlberg et al., 2013) – a way of ensuring that early years providers are on a path to achieve the desired outcomes. Monitoring is about ensuring that leaders and practitioners do not depart from what has been constructed as the norm. For policy makers, it is about a hegemonic system (see Chapter 1), rather than one that embraces innovation (Dahlberg and Moss, 2005). Therefore, inspection regimes act as a **panoptic gaze**.

The panoptic gaze draws from the work of Foucault (1995) where he explored the panopticon, a circular building with an observation tower in the middle whereby those in the middle can observe all that is happening in the circular building. Foucault discusses this model in regard to prisons, but we can apply the principles to inspection and monitoring systems in other disciplines, such as early years, and without the physicality of the building. If you view those who do the monitoring as being in the tower and all early years practitioners as being in the circular building, you can see how the symbolism implies that inspection and monitoring generate a feeling of being watched at all times. The monitoring of provision is not a problem in itself – it is important to regulate providers, particularly when taking into account child protection. What we are concerned about is that the inspection and monitoring process assumes a set of collective objectives, a shared view as to the role of early years services, but it is not transparent what the objectives are. Dahlberg and Moss (2005) and Dahlberg et al. (2013) discuss that quality assessments are not value neutral, but nor are the values self-evident.

In considering policy as a series of discourses, we are able to reflect on how they seek to shape early years practice. However, it is also evident how policy makers look to render some features of early years practice invisible (Mitchell, 2010). There is a suggestion that policy makers can identify a problem, find the solution in a scientific and rational way and that the one solution will fit many contexts and be unproblematic (Blackmore, 1995). The example of the providers who feel they have achieved quality by gaining an Outstanding grade from Ofsted indicates the risk of no longer considering what it is that led to that Outstanding grade – why it is that you do what you do as an early years practitioner and leader. Accepting one way of doing things and not questioning this will result in only one way of doing things, as there will be no reflective process to consider how to continually develop early years practice. Yet, stop to think about early years providers and it is evident that there are differences in how settings seek to develop the quality of their practice. It is not like going to a supermarket where there is a predictable layout of food – whilst there are common features in early years settings, they are characterised by variation. Dahlberg and Moss (2005) discuss the work of Loris Malaguzzi and Reggio Emilia and the concept of 100 Languages of Children – children have multiple ways of communicating and we, as practitioners, have to be adept at listening to and hearing them. The idea of 100 Languages is also about how there are 100 ways to define and implement understandings of quality early years practice.

For us, this variation in how quality is constructed by individuals is not just about recognising the limits of a supposedly objective quality monitoring system like Ofsted or pushing against the power dynamics, it is also about finding your voice. In adopting a post-structuralist perspective of quality, quality tools and frameworks do not have to be about uniformity. Quality is complex, as are the children that attend early years services. As we discuss in Chapter 6, early years practitioners have a long history of reflecting on their working practices and observing the children that they work with to inform their practice. This reflection process can aid the deconstruction process. The implementation of any quality guidance tool or framework requires a process of interpretation. In interpreting quality guidance, you can find your voice to develop a sense of quality that is meaningful to you and the children that you work with. As a practitioner, you have social agency. **Social agency** is the ability to make free choices and not be subject to constraining social structures. Social agency provides you with the ability not just to react to policy directives, but to look at them and interpret them in ways that are meaningful for your setting (Osgood, 2006). Given this, we now begin to consider what it is that parents and children think about quality early years provision, as this will be part of how you interpret guidance documents.

Parental Perspectives on Quality

Parental understandings of quality are somewhat debated as there is the suggestion that parents do not always have an understanding of what quality early years provision looks like. For example, research into the views of Greek parents suggests that they overestimate quality (Grammatikopoulos et al., 2014); Mathers et al.'s (2012) study, referred to earlier, suggests that parents do not understand Ofsted reports; and Huskins et al. (2014) found that parents lacked an understanding of the EYFS. However, this perception is based on one particular view of quality. To say that a parent does not understand an Ofsted report is not to say that they do not understand quality; it is just that version of quality which is unclear to them, raising questions as to the differing perspectives of relevance.

One way to see how parents view early years provision is to look at how they choose the setting their child will attend. The choice agenda is about citizens becoming consumers (particularly in a mixed-market model) and thereby driving the quality of services (Clarke et al., 2005). The intensification of the role of markets in social policy sees the state as stimulating the market (Krieger, 2007), but giving the responsibility to citizens to shape service provision. Parental choice will determine which settings are desirable and regarded to be of good quality. However, there is little evidence to support the belief that parental choice regulates the quality of provision (OECD, 2006). We have already seen that parents find Ofsted reports hard to understand, but there is also evidence that they look for different features of quality, leading to highly personal definitions of the term that are impossible to reduce to a simple set of national, measurable variables.

When we look at research evidence on what parents feel is important for early years provision (often based on how they have gone about choosing early years provision), we can see that, perhaps unsurprisingly, they focus on the more emotional features that we found in the early years providers referred to earlier. Mathers et al. (2012) provide some detail in regard to how parents look for warm, nurturing environments where children are emotionally secure. A survey in 2010 found that 'well qualified, trained or experienced' staff was also important and that parents were more likely to consider the staffing, or the cost of care, than the Ofsted report in selecting a setting to use (Daycare Trust, 2010). Parents also look for adults who support a child's learning, respond to their needs and support interactions between children (Huskins et al., 2014). Evidence from Hungary suggests that English parents are not alone in looking for emotional aspects, with Brayfield and Korintus (2011) finding Hungarian parents citing child-loving adults as the most important aspect of early years provision. Trust also comes out as an important feature of early years provider choice (Vincent et al., 2008). The suggestion from the research evidence is that following practical considerations, it is the staff that influence parental views on the quality of care. Yet, it is not the qualification level of a member of staff that is considered, but their approach to their work, and this is very hard to quantify.

The Childcare and Early Years Survey of Parents is a survey that has been undertaken on behalf of the Department for Education for more than ten years.

Whilst the questions have varied each year, it provides us with a longitudinal overview of how parents choose their childcare provision – the elements that are important to them. In the latest survey, the provider's reputation is cited as the most important feature, followed by convenience and then quality (Huskins et al., 2014). The difficulty with a survey such as this is that we do not know what respondents think constitutes a good reputation. Vincent et al. (2008) conducted qualitative research in London, exploring parental childcare choices, and found that parents are shaped by the communities in which they live. It is not just that recommendations influence the early years provision that a parent will choose, but communities also shape how parents understand the role and purpose of early years services. Vincent et al. (2008) consider social class as an influence on childcare choices – in part, the choice is related to the socio-economics of the family, so factors such as cost and employment patterns act as a practical influence on the choice of childcare. However, social groupings also create cultures of motherhood whereby shared norms and values around early years provision are created. For example, parents who work will often be friends with other parents who work and will have shared views on the importance of childcare in supporting their work patterns. Other parents may choose to stay at home whilst their children are young, so their choice of early years provider will be shaped by a different set of needs and values. There is therefore a complex interaction between the practicalities of early years provision and the cultural construction of the use of early years provision. Understandings of what constitutes a good childhood, a good family life and a good parent will all interplay with practical considerations to determine how or if a family uses early years provision. Yet research has shown that the process of deciding to use early years provision is a fluid one and subject to change as children's needs change (Ellison et al., 2009). Of course, parental choice might not always be a completely free one – parents can be severely constrained by availability and cost – and, equally, policy initiatives might seek to influence the behaviour of parents, such as putting sanctions in place for lone parents on benefits to ensure that they actively look for employment. In particular, we see the influence of gender norms on parental choices, with fathers indicating that they would like to have more opportunities to spend increased amounts of time with their children, whilst women feel that they carry the burden of childcare arrangements (Ellison et al., 2009).

The Early Years Market and Parental Choice

Parental choice, when looking at the quality of provision, can also be constrained by the mixed economy of providers. The maintained sector is routinely demonstrated to have higher levels of quality, both when looking at Ofsted grades and in other research such as EPPE. Yet despite this, many **neo-liberal governments** (such as the UK) rely on the private sector to provide early years provision. Neo-liberal governments are those that have moved away from a system of the state (the government) providing services towards a system of a free-market economy. There is a long history and much debate on the development of neo-liberal governments, but what is of interest here is the existence of the free-market economy, so rather than the government providing early years services we see a range of private sector, independent, voluntary and some maintained providers offering early years services. The focus on the market for supplying early years services was evident in the National Childcare Strategy in the UK, where there was a clear emphasis on supporting private providers to meet the shortfall in places. The UK is not the only country with such a system as other countries, such as Australia, Hong Kong and the Netherlands, have adopted similar models (Campbell-Barr, 2014).

The concerns expressed about relying on markets vary depending on who is looking at them. As we have seen, governments introduce accountability structures to ensure that the market is meeting policy objectives. Governments also try to develop discursive truths as to how early years providers should operate in the market – managerial and entrepreneurial – in order to address concerns around sustainability (Campbell-Barr, 2014). But there are other, more ethical concerns that can be raised when considering non-governmental perspectives. One criticism is that markets are focused on profits and not quality (Goodfellow, 2005), therefore profits will serve the interests of shareholders and/or owners rather than being reinvested into the quality of provision. In particular, there is anxiety in both the UK (Lloyd and Penn, 2010) and Australia (Sumsion, 2006) that growth in large corporate chains could result in the substantial loss of an underlying ethic of care as early years providers become more focused on the managerial and entrepreneurial aspects of their role. If profits serve the interests of owners, then it undermines a model that assumes that the market will drive up quality. Such a model assumes that as parents choose good quality provision, the profits made by the early years provider will be reinvested in the quality of provision. The evidence reviewed above regarding the emotional aspects of early years provision suggests that providers are resistant to an erosion of an ethic of care and that many are still guided by the needs of the child, and our experiences are that there are many providers who remain focused on the child and reinvest profit into the quality of provision, but we will return to the tensions between care and **managerialism** in Chapters 4 and 5.

There is also the question of whether or not parental choice improves quality as it may be that parents are not the best judges of quality or that they do not judge quality in the same way as policy makers or other stakeholders. Being the most popular early years provider does not automatically equate to being the best quality provider. Further, in areas where there is little provision, quality may not feature in parental choice as it becomes an issue of using what is available. Cleveland et al. (2007) researching in Canada have explored the difference in the quality of provision between for-profit and not-for-profit providers. The relationship to other neo-liberal markets for this piece of research needs to be treated with some caution as there are issues with how the authors identify for-profit status, but it leads to some interesting insights into how markets operate. Cleveland et al. find that it is not the for-profit status of providers that is important for determining quality, but the nature of the market in which they are operating. They describe markets as thick (high levels of competition amongst consumers for places) or thin. They find that looking at the market in this way highlights how not-for-profit providers are able to respond to the area that they are in. They hypothesise that in thin markets there is no opportunity for not-for-profit providers to differentiate themselves as the pressure is on filling places. However, in thick markets, not-for-profit providers can charge higher fees and aim for a higher quality service.

Child Views on Quality

The research evidence on child perceptions of quality early years provision is limited. It might be that practitioners are engaged in seeking child perceptions of quality every day, but the evidence is not being published. In the same way that the reasons for investing in early years services by governments that we discussed in the previous chapter tell us a lot about how we conceptualise children and childhood, so too does the lack of published research on children's perceptions of the early years services that they are attending. Given that it is children who attend early years settings, it would seem fundamental that we include their voices in constructions of quality, but at present their perspectives are limited by the level of available evidence. Children were involved in the early iteration of Every Child Matters (DfES, 2004) in the UK where they were asked what mattered to them, with the findings being used to develop a set of guiding principles for the development of policy for children's services (not just those pertaining to the early years). Two things stand out in this process: (1) the research was done with children aged over 8 years on the premise that younger children would not know what mattered to them; and (2) 'have fun' was used by the children (see below for a further mention of the concept of fun in relation to what children regard as quality in their setting) but was changed by policy makers at the time to 'enjoy and achieve' (Sinclair, 2004), giving us a clear indication of the discourse of children as 'becoming' rather than 'being'.

Mooney and Blackburn (2003) conducted one of the few pieces of research with children in a range of early education and childcare services in London and the south-east of England to explore their views on quality. They found that children valued their friends, that they wanted settings to be fun, with a range of activities and equipment, and that they enjoyed having access to the outside. Children also discussed food – not just in regard to what they ate, but also in terms of eating being a social activity. Caring, friendly, helpful and playful staff were also important to the children and they did not like it when staff spent too much time in the office or were just talking amongst themselves. The findings are limited to the small sample size (62 children), but much of what Mooney and Blackburn found feels as if it would be relevant for other children today. What is interesting is that whilst there are some overlaps with quality indicators in the Ofsted framework, ECERS and parental perspectives, the findings give some important messages about how children see early years services – as fun, friendly, warm and sociable.

Coleyshaw et al. (2012) explored the different ways in which early years providers engage with the views of children: (1) they facilitate their choice; (2) they consult with children; (3) they co-construct. In these three approaches, we can see a continuum of engagement with the voice of the child. Interestingly, those settings that were seen as being less hierarchical in their approach to leadership were found to be those most likely to seek to co-construct understandings of quality in early years settings (Coleyshaw et al., 2012). Sommer et al. (2013) explore how early years practitioners need to respond to children's utterances in order to understand them and their experiences. However, as they further point out, the difficulty is that often the child's perspective is seen as being external to the child as it is constructed by an adult. One of the difficulties is that policy makers create a view of the child as becoming – a child that is valued on the basis of the adult they will become in the future. In viewing the child as becoming, it does not position the child in an early years setting as having a sense of agency whereby they may contribute to understandings of quality. However, we know from our experiences of working with early years providers that they *do* see children as having social agency. We know that they listen to children and respond to their needs on a daily basis and we would suggest that this is fundamental to developing an understanding of quality.

Your Views on Quality

Having considered the different views on quality that have been presented in this chapter and in Chapter 1, we have identified that understandings of quality early years services are shaped by many factors and that these will depend on who it is that is constructing the purpose and related quality of provision. Global, national, early years leader, practitioner, parent and child viewpoints all come together to shape and inform perspectives on quality early years services. Often, stakeholders have different understandings of quality and its importance that come from their different belief systems.

As we have outlined in this chapter, policy makers look to utilise power relationships within society to shape understandings of why early years services are important and how quality is conceptualised. However, what we hope we have demonstrated in this chapter is that there are different interpretations of early years services and quality. Quality is a complex mix of structural and process features that, on the one hand, will favour modernist approaches to elements of quality that can be measured and assessed, but on the other, reflect the less tangible aspects – often the more dispositional and emotional features that act to guide leaders and practitioners in developing the quality of early years services and which influence parents in their choices. We feel that there is still more to be done to develop understandings of child perspectives, but the features that we have identified from them – having fun, being friendly and sociable – are an important starting point for guiding quality early years provision.

What we also appreciate is that as a leader, developing the quality of an early years setting can feel challenging as you find yourself negotiating between different stakeholder perspectives. We will focus on this in more detail in Chapters 3 and 4. However, what we want to consider here is how post-structuralist perspectives encourage us to find the cracks in the structures that we are presented with, such as quality frameworks, and how to find ways to work within these cracks. Accountability structures do not mean one size fits all and a hegemonic approach to quality early years services. Therefore, how you understand quality today may be different to what you thought last week or last year. Equally, how you view quality when working in one setting might differ from other settings that you have worked in, as quality should be meaningful to the context that you are in. Given this, it is important that you think about what you regard as quality, but that you do this in relation to why you think these features are important, noting that this will relate to why you think early years services are important.

WHAT IS QUALITY? EXPLORING THE EVIDENCE BASE 43

> **Reflection Point**
>
> Figure 2.1 offers a summary of the features of quality that we have identified in this chapter from a range of stakeholders. As you look at the figure, think about your own views on quality. How would you position each of the features – which ones would come first and why? Would any be larger than the others? Would you leave any out?

Figure 2.1 Aspects of quality early years provision

We have intentionally highlighted staffing in Figure 2.1 as this is an aspect of quality that re-occurs in our discussion, but it also has considerable range in terms of what it is about staff that is seen to be important. What we have not included in the figure is anything on leadership. We have seen in this chapter that there is evidence that leadership relates to the ways in which practitioners engage with the views of children, but there is obviously more to leadership than just listening to children, as we will consider in depth in the next two chapters.

Chapter Summary

- Regulation systems are just one view of quality. The variation in early years providers highlights that there are different ways to interpret regulation requirements.
- Practitioners and parents favour more emotional features of quality than those evident in official assessments.
- Children want fun, friendly and sociable early years settings.
- Post-structuralism enables you to question who is constructing understandings of quality, how they have constructed them and how you can deconstruct them to develop an understanding of quality that is meaningful for you and the children that you work with.

Further Reading

Cottle, M. and Alexander, E. (2012) 'Quality in early years settings: government, research and practitioners' perspectives', *British Educational Research Journal*, 38 (4): 635–54.

In this article, the authors focus on the views of early years practitioners and how they adopt policy ideas about what quality means, while acknowledging that often practitioners find themselves with internal tensions in developing an understanding of quality.

Vincent, C., Braun, A. and Ball, S. J. (2008) 'Childcare, choice and social class: caring for young children in the UK', *Critical Social Policy*, 28 (1): 5–26.

In this article, the authors consider how parents can live geographically very close together, but have different social networks and relationships with early years services.

PART TWO
LEADERSHIP

TRACING THE DEVELOPMENT OF EARLY YEARS LEADERSHIP

> **Chapter Overview**
>
> In this chapter, we look more deeply at how leadership has historically been expressed in early years settings and how it has subsequently developed in terms of possible models to inspire today's leaders. We explore the shift from concentration on the qualities and characteristics that leaders embody to acknowledgement of the importance of the context of leadership. We also note the growth of formalised leadership education and training (NCSL, 2004) which has helped create an awareness of the unique nature of leading early years settings.

As stated in our Introduction, we have consistently seen research and subsequent policy development that firmly situate leadership as a key attribute of achieving and sustaining quality provision for children and families (Aubrey, 2007; Rodd, 2012). Leadership in the early years sector is relatively new with a history of over twenty years of research and academic study both nationally (Aubrey, 2007; Dunlop, 2008; Rodd, 2012) and internationally (Heikka and Waniganayake, 2011; Ho, 2012). Whilst we have already outlined the challenges of looking at research on quality in the previous two chapters, research to date has routinely shown the positive impact of leadership on the quality of settings (Sylva et al., 2004). This knowledge has led to demands for improvement in the leadership capacity of individuals at all levels of an organisation, especially at the top. Furthermore, an expectation has been created that a leader will take full responsibility for the actions of their staff, alongside the education outcomes of the children engaged with their services, as is evident in the accountability models that we discussed in Chapter 2.

Early Experiences of Leadership in Early Years Settings

As we explored in Chapter 1, there is a long and complex history to the development of early years services in the UK (and other parts of the world). The history of how services have developed is important as services shape not only the structure of the early years sector, such as the different types of early years providers and who works in them, but also the philosophy underpinning the services. Key to our discussion on leadership is how historically there was little interest in how leadership was expressed in early years settings and there were no obvious drivers to establish a leadership culture in what was perceived as a voluntary, self-driven service for highly localised communities. It is well documented that early years provision during the 1960s and 1970s was regarded as a wholly female domain (Campbell-Barr, 2009a; Hard and O'Gorman, 2007; Leeson, 2014; Osgood, 2012; Woodrow and Busch, 2008) and this perception has barely changed (Harwood et al., 2013; Osgood, 2012; Rodd, 2012). As a consequence, early years work became characterised as low level, low paid and undervalued, only performed by women and regarded as a simple extension of their role as mothers (Taggart, 2011), with the assumption that they were able to utilise their innate caring skills. That belief has essentially changed very little (McDowall Clark and Baylis, 2012) and we might argue that early years has always been regarded as a female occupation with a predominantly female workforce and with wages, terms and conditions that have not improved substantially, despite the increased expectations placed on settings in terms of early education and full day care for working families. Furthermore, the poor terms and conditions mean that leaders are frequently unable to access any leadership training/education or have time off to study and develop their skills. It is therefore understandable that leaders of settings and their workforce have tended to believe that their role is minimal, their impact is perceived as unimportant except in situations where things have gone wrong and they are disregarded and undervalued by large sectors of the community.

The first early years settings were based around play for children and support for parents (predominantly mothers) in a community or church centre. The belief of the time was that 'real' learning took place once the child started school with what was regarded as a properly trained and professional workforce; thus, what happened before the age of 5 was not and did not need to be viewed as anything other than an opportunity for socialisation and occupation. As we outlined in Chapter 1, this divide between childcare (primarily to support working and 'in-need' parents) and early education has been something that global organisations have looked to limit, and certainly in the UK we have seen support for a model of 'educare'. The educare model has clear consequences for understandings of leadership, but so too has the related interest in the role of early years services. The growth in interest in the provision of early years services and the desire to secure 'quality' early years provision have resulted in a greater emphasis being placed on the existence of effective leadership. Consequently, we see politicians, economists and the business sector begin to make demands for greater professionalisation and accountability of leaders of early years settings (McDowall Clark and Baylis, 2012).

In the UK, the focus on leadership of early years settings began to grow in the 1990s when influential reports started to discuss the importance of early learning and the settings in which this happened (Evangelou et al., 2009). Policy and practice began to highlight issues relating to the high quality of early years provision and raise questions as to who the leaders of settings were and how they might best lead to ensure good learning opportunities for young children. This upscaling of the role was not going to be without its problems – leaders did not recognise themselves as such (Rodd, 2006; Torrance, 2013). They had been positioned as caring women helping their fellow women raise their children and had embraced that identity. The formation of a discourse of deficiency emerged that underpinned early years provision; that services existed to 'make up for' what the child is not getting in the home helped further the belief of the early years workforce, supporting their sisters in caring for their children. Yet the deficiency model, whereby early years services act as a social investment to equal the life chances of children (see Chapter 1), feels contradictory to the market model that is evident in many neo-liberal economies (as discussed in Chapter 2). The former focuses on the needs of the child and the latter on profits. The deficiency model reflects the fear that market models could result in a loss of an ethic of care that we discussed in Chapter 2, but, as we also identified, it is often the case that early years providers intend to combine an ethic of care with *managerialist* agendas. Here we see that leaders are asked to hold these two discourses in tension in a situation which is increasingly complex to manage – we will discuss this further in Chapter 4.

Thus, it would seem that the plethora of reports and heightened public and political interest in the quality of leadership in the sector have been at odds with the daily experience of early years leaders. The political movements to develop early years services and create more places by inviting a mixed economy of providers and to link provision more closely with education systems and structures, meant that the workforce would need support and direction to make the changes being demanded as it became accepted that they were unlikely to manage the transition themselves. Therefore, effective leadership became identified as a key factor in determining the value and worth of an individual setting and the collective field. However, early pioneers had only business models of leadership to inform their newly formed leadership practice (Rodd, 1998), where managerial tasks were regarded as the most important aspects of the role and personality traits of competitiveness and assertiveness were seen as more desirable than collegiality and consultative practice. Discussions about whether leadership and management roles should be regarded as separate or integral (Adair, 1973; Hall, 1996; Murray and McDowall Clark, 2013; Owen, 2000) have led to increased tensions between the two with little or no agreement as to their relationship with each other. Thus, business models of leadership have been treated with caution by leaders in the care and education sectors and have tended to be regarded as unhelpful as we try to manage the ambivalence which lies at the heart of leading a setting. For example, many tensions have been experienced when playgroup committees have tried to exert some authority through business-like frameworks of leading and managing and attempted to 'bring order' to the proceedings of a setting, often much to the frustration of an experienced and highly competent leader who understands the needs of the children and regards the actions of the committee as inappropriate and unhelpful. It became evident that a different landscape was needed that early years leaders could identify with and embrace.

Heikka and Waniganayake (2011) regard the move away from these traditional, modernist models of leadership as a key turning point for the early years sector where we began to recognise that the task was more than the rational, objective tasks of management or administration and to look for leadership models that were more pedagogical, relational, holistic and focused on learning and caring. For a brief time, educational leadership models became the primary resource for inspiration where a substantial literature existed to inform practice in what, at first glance, might be considered a similar, educational domain, but these models were soon deemed inadequate given the uniqueness of early years leadership with its high concentration on relationships, empowerment and community nourishment (Leeson, 2010).

Influential Leadership Theories

Leadership theories can be broadly categorised as transactional (trait and style theories); transformational (distributed leadership, transformational, authentic); and heroic (entrepreneurial) leadership theories (see Table 3.1).

Table 3.1 Table of leadership theory

Leadership development	Key leadership theories	Position of leader	Power structure	Ownership of vision	Characteristics
Transactional leadership	Trait theories Style theories	Leader at centre (hub and spoke concept)	Leader has most power; all communication comes through leader	Communicates leader's vision	Managerialist Administrative Adaptable A modernist, rational and scientific base
Transformational leadership	Distributed leadership Entrepreneurial team	Leader as part of the line A 'flat' or linear hierarchy	Leader shares power	Creates shared vision	Relational Holistic Post-structural base of co-construction and dialogue
Heroic leadership	Entrepreneurial leader Trait theories Style theories Distributed leadership	Leader at the top A hierarchical pyramid structure	Leader has power though may distribute where necessary/valuable	Creates a culture of vision	Charismatic May be seen as manipulative Post-structural in terms of creativity and challenge, but may also be seen as modernist in terms of privileging a rational and scientific view of the market

Source: Adapted from Metcalfe and Metcalfe's (2008) three stages of leadership development

Trait and style theories

Early leadership theories such as trait theories and style theories are modernist in nature as they are scientific, rational and highly predictable. Trait theories have been hugely influential and have been regarded as particularly helpful as they offer effective signposts for identifying a person's leadership potential (Davis, 2012). Indeed, trait theory formed the basis of most leadership research during the early twentieth century with various attempts being made to identify the desirable personality traits or personal characteristics, which would indicate an individual's suitability as a leader, such as emotional stability, extraversion and conscientiousness (Cattell, 1966). These traits formed the basis for various psychometric tests to determine an individual's suitability for a specific leadership position within an organisation.

Thus, in a modernist world, the facility to assess a person's potential for leadership has been attractive as providing some certainty through its predictive quality. Its strong heritage of believing in innate leadership also meant that, not only would it enable the selection of the right individual but it would mean a saving on training as the successful candidate would already possess the desired attributes or the innate capacity to develop them without too much intervention or support. For early years, trait theory could be problematic as the traits that dominate the landscape were derived from studies of successful leaders in history such as Julius Caesar, Alexander the Great, Mahatma Gandhi and Martin Luther King. Only recently have there been studies on the leadership traits of female leaders such as Boudicca, Anita Roddick and Margaret Thatcher to give balance and explore the full panoply of leadership examples. Although it is now regarded as simplistic to attribute traits as masculine or feminine and research has shown that leaders are able to access a wide variety of these traits irrespective of their classification, the gendered nature of traits still dominates the theoretical landscape, inhibiting the development of professional zeal – the passionate care that has always characterised early years practice (Murray and McDowall Clark, 2013). Despite criticism that trait theories are limited and simplistic, they remain influential though now they are most often referred to as non-conscious drivers that influence our behaviour. Certainly, considerable research energy has been given to establishing the traits that would be desirable in early years leaders, leading to a number of key traits or dispositions being identified, such as:

- being an effective communicator (Siraj-Blatchford and Manni, 2007; Sylva et al., 2004)
- being authentic (Curtis and Burton, 2009; Jones and Pound, 2008; Moyles, 2006; Sylva et al., 2004; West-Burnham et al., 2007)

- being able to inspire others (Earley and Weindling, 2004; Jones and Pound, 2008; Moyles, 2006; Siraj-Blatchford and Manni, 2007; West-Burnham et al., 2007).

Within the wider field of leadership theory, the identification of key traits has led to substantial debate as to whether these traits are innate (reflecting the dispositions discussed in Chapter 2) or learnt, with many tools being developed to explore natural dispositional leadership behaviour as well as a plethora of training programmes to draw them out and teach those traits identified as possible to learn. Anxieties that trait theories were too simplistic and a growing awareness of the context of leadership led to the development of a typology of leadership styles – once again to facilitate the predictive capacity of large organisations to establish who would be best for any particular leadership positions (Blake and Moulton, 1964).

Situational and contingency theories

One may be concerned about the perceived lack of authenticity within the situational or contingency group of style theories. The ability to choose a different style of working in different situations could be regarded as false, playing a 'game'; leading to difficulties in grasping the authenticity of the individual – an important aspect of strong, enduring and helpful relationships (Rogers, 1951). Others have argued that style theories have their merit and their place as important leadership models as they offer mechanisms for understanding how best to handle particular situations, together with a mindfulness of the stance of being the leader (Telford, 1996). With style theories, the focus became how leaders behaved, with dozens of leadership styles being identified by many writers who used different words to describe essentially similar behaviours. Some key style theories that have helped in the development of early years leadership theory are the work of Likert (1967), Tannenbaum and Schmidt (1958) and Hersey and Blanchard (1977). A further modernist, rational and technical approach to leadership is that of Likert where he identifies four different leadership styles that he saw as being fixed. A leader would possess the attributes to lead using only one of these styles and would not have the capacity to move between them depending on the situation they found themselves in, but just as modernist approaches to quality ask questions of what falls outside of the classifications (see Chapter 1), so do Likert's classifications. His classifications are as follows:

- exploitative/authoritarian, where leaders tell their subordinates what to do and expect to be obeyed without question
- benevolent/authoritarian, where leaders take responsibility for being in charge and have a paternalistic approach/manner towards their employees
- consultative leadership, where employees are asked their opinion prior to decision making
- participative, where employees are fully involved in decision-making processes.

Hersey and Blanchard also identified four leadership styles, but argued that theirs were more flexible, enabling leaders to use different styles to lead in different situations, taking account of the tasks that needed to be done along with the relationships between the leader and others in the organisation. Their theory, along with others of a similar ilk, became sub-classified as situational or contingency leadership. Their leadership styles were:

- telling – used where the task is repetitive or needs doing quickly
- selling – to encourage and motivate people to do the tasks required
- participating – staff competence is high, but they are not fully cognizant of their expertise or sufficiently confident in it so tasks still need the facilitation, supervision and support of the leader
- delegating – strong staff motivation and competence mean that they can get on with the task without supervision or direct support of the leader.

Situational leadership requires leaders to be skilful at reading the contexts they find themselves in and selecting the right leadership style to get the most out of the situation and their staff – what Fiedler and Chemers (1974) term 'leader match'. A concept of 'best fit' emerged where leaders were able to be chosen by an organisation looking for an effective leader for a particular situation given the structure of the task, the characteristics of all the people involved, both leaders and led, and the nature and quality of the relationship between them. Such theories encourage us to look differently at the relationship between leaders and their context; to consider the impact of the situation on the leader rather than the leader's impact on the situation (Northouse, 2010). What is also worth noting is that situational/contingency theories of leadership create the first opportunity to accept that leaders do not have to be effective in all situations (Northouse, 2010).

Tannenbaum and Schmidt (1958) were interested in decision-making processes and identified a spectrum of situations and styles that could be used to identify what leadership style would be required in what situation. Their spectrum proved useful to an understanding of the complexities of leadership and that over time leaders might be required to move from one style to another as their teams and tasks changed. Early years leadership theory has been considerably influenced by style theories. For example, Neugebauer (1985), who has been variously cited by influential theorists such as Rodd (1998), identified specific early years styles of leadership such as the Task Master, the Comrade, the Motivator and the Unleader and suggested that the third was the most effective. Style theorists such as Neugebauer, Hersey and Blanchard made an extremely significant contribution to the development of a theory of early years leadership as they emphasised the central importance of context to effective leadership. Context continues to be an important aspect of early years leadership, the leadership style being that which works best within the parameters of the setting and the community it serves (Fleer, 2003; Tobin, 2005).

The New Leadership Paradigm

Nevertheless, all of these early theories have ultimately been found wanting by many working in the early years as they concentrate too much on the characteristics of the leader themselves rather than on the relational context in which they lead. To address concerns over the lack of interest in the *context* of leadership, courses such as the National Professional Qualification in Integrated Centre Leadership, based on work by the Pen Green Leadership Centre, were designed, concentrating on capturing and bringing forth those natural dispositions within a context of encouraging the creative exploration of the self as leader, as well as offering tools and strategies for leadership. Such programmes promoted and supported a new leadership focus on the actions of leaders rather than their attributes, moving from thinking about the leader themselves to thinking about the situations in which leadership occurs. Thus, post-structural dissatisfaction with the limitations of style and trait theories, as well as the desire to establish a leadership philosophy that was discursive and privileged the relational complexities of the leadership task, led to an investigation of the new leadership **paradigm** (Northouse, 2010) where relationships are clearly situated at the centre of leadership activities. Considering the research evidence on what early years practitioners deem important for quality provision (see Chapter 2), it is possible to identify their more emotional features – the new leadership paradigm is thus a better fit with the original identity of nurturing and supporting children and parents. We would suggest that the new leadership paradigm is reflective of the shift away from modernist approaches to quality towards post-structuralist understandings. Just as we outlined in Chapter 1, there was a dissatisfaction with modernist approaches to quality as they felt too restrictive and imposed onto the sector rather than constructed with it. The same can be said of leadership models that emphasise the managerial elements of the task. The new leadership paradigm is, therefore, in contrast to a model where leaders are subject to the panoptic gaze. Leadership becomes less about applying the right techniques at the right times in order to achieve the desired outcomes and more about a focus on the relational features identified as important aspects of quality for early years providers, parents and children. Transformational styles of leadership that focused on working together towards shared goals (Burns, 1978) paved the way for the development of theories that encouraged the creation of emotionally literate and sensitively responsive environments, which required leaders who were aware of their own emotions, were committed to professionalism and were empowering, trusting and optimistic (Goleman et al., 2002; McBride and Maitland, 2002). A key aspect of transformational leadership theories is their people-oriented approach that focuses on hearts and minds, empowering staff to learn and to seek change and personal improvement, not controlling them or telling them what to do.

Just as Adair (1973), looked to motivational theory to inform his model of action-centred leadership transformational theories borrow heavily from Maslow's hierarchy of needs and seek to create an environment in which people can feel safe, respected and develop their own potential as well as that of others. Transformational theories indicate an important move away from a focus on outcomes and seek to enable all who work within the organisation to feel able to trust those with whom they work, knowing they have an impact on the culture of the organisation, thereby developing a sense of ownership and an awareness of their own leadership capacity (Owen, 2000). Nias et al. (1989) were among the first to see leadership as a collaborative process wherein leaders and led have shared values, beliefs and attitudes that help them towards shared goals. Thus, discourse that sees leadership as innate – the born leader – is at odds with the strong discourse of all of us having leadership potential (Aubrey, 2007; Owen, 2000; Rodd, 2012; Telford, 1996). A key aspect of transformational leadership is the idea that we all have leadership capacity and it is the responsibility of the leader to assist us in realising this potential. It certainly underpins the theory of distributed leadership which sees leadership as moving throughout the layers and situations within a setting – moving away from a traditional hierarchical approach to leadership towards one of shared responsibility. Such a shift enables the development of singular models of leadership that are highly contextualised and unique. The building blocks mentioned in Chapter 1 are relevant here; the different ways in which the blocks might be constructed, taken apart and rebuilt gives great flexibility to the leadership of responsive and effective settings.

Distributed leadership has been very popular with government and key writers in early years leadership as offering a human capital, transformational perspective that encourages all employees to take ownership and responsibility for the way an organisation is led and to develop the leadership capacity of workers who might not be aware of those skills within themselves. Policy makers, in particular, talk a great deal about the desirability of certain aspects of distributed leadership across the early years sector and have promoted it through various documents, policy development and training strategies (Hadfield et al., 2010). Ho (2012), writing in the context of Hong Kong, argues that distributed leadership should allow leaders to think more about a leadership team rather than focusing on the individual, which enables shared power, responsibility and accountability. Others are similarly impressed with the flexibility that distributed leadership offers and its move away from a focus on the leader as an individual with particular skills and attributes towards the effective sharing of tasks that need to be done (Earley and Weindling, 2004). Likewise, Aubrey (2007) feels that distributed leadership allows for collaboration, interaction and interdependence and thus the development of powerful and sustainable learning communities.

Distributed leadership is not without its critics, however. A key criticism is that, in order for distributed leadership to work, the hierarchical leader has to champion it and take specific steps to ensure it happens, which encourages other members of the organisation to regard it as the 'gift' of the leader as opposed to a right and therefore not as democratic as an initial investigation would suggest (Torrance, 2013). Thus, Torrance argues, distributed leadership is not as flexible or transportable as its adherents would wish; instead, it is highly context-specific and hierarchical. It would seem that the close supervision of distributed leadership operations may make busy leaders feel that it is easier, quicker and more efficient to do tasks themselves as issues of responsibility and accountability are not clear. Given the close link between quality provision and better outcomes for children, questions must be asked as to how comfortable a leader will feel in handing full responsibility to other staff members. Wright (2008) feels that distributed leadership could be viewed as an opportunity for leaders to get rid of the more boring administrative tasks to other staff members and that it is therefore not really about leadership. Furthermore, there is concern that distributed leadership has created a tyranny with its assumption that everyone wants to lead, which means that those who wish simply to be led are unable to opt out of having a leadership role forced upon them. Thus, distributed leadership should be treated with caution and carefully considered as it may cause tension, friction and anxiety.

Entrepreneurial Leadership

A government preference for simple solutions to complex issues has led to the promotion of a one-size-fits-all style of leadership, most commonly derived from managerialist, rational and technical models of leadership with 'superhero' charismatic individuals at the helm seeking as flexible and transportable a style of leadership as possible, allowing control and creating a high degree of predictable success. Just as understandings of quality have become about the one model of quality that negates cultural understandings of children, childhood and early years services, the same can be said of leadership. Yet the relationship between quality and leadership extends beyond this. In Chapter 2, we discussed the reliance on the market to provide early years services in neo-liberal economies. Policy makers have worked hard to mould the character of the early years market to ensure that it meets policy objectives and is sustainable. Leading with emotions does not fit with the managerialist agendas of policy makers and can pose a threat to the sustainability of services as emotions do not make good business sense. Writers such as Osgood (2004, 2006) and Campbell-Barr (2009a) have written about how policy has tried to mould early years provision along entrepreneurial lines. As a result, entrepreneurial leadership has emerged with a predilection for a particular model of entrepreneurialism that promotes the concept of an individual hero who will address all the issues and make everything perfect. This preferred model of leadership has the added benefit that entrepreneurs are commonly regarded as extremely skilled at doing more for less in straitened economic circumstances. Entrepreneurial leaders are usually characterised as charismatic, powerful and confident people with strong internal drives for achievement and control (Bolton and Thompson, 2004; Garvey and Lancaster, 2010; Vecchio, 2003), which are attractive qualities for any government intent on reasserting modernist values of predictability and scientific certainty. Indeed, there have been a number of high-profile success stories in the early years sector for a number of years (the 4children website has a store of such stories, see www.4children.org.uk/Resources/Detail/Case-Study-Dragon-Fishers as an example), which encourage the perception of effective early years leaders as heroic, special people who not only embody strong leadership, but have created effective, financially successful businesses through their efforts. An added attraction of these superheroes, for policy makers, is that they can be moved from one location to another, utilising their skills to develop settings that have been found wanting in their achievements or their quality ratings. However, a key problem with entrepreneurial leaders is that they often leave the role after making major changes, leaving behind them unresolved issues and difficulties (Bolden et al., 2011) that then have to be addressed. It would appear that there are serious difficulties in the wholesale transportation, usually with the minimum of reflection, of that which works well in one environment to another that is highly likely to be very different in physical structure, staffing and community expectation. Another problem with this construction of the entrepreneurial leader is that they are usually difficult to emulate and the literature on incomplete leadership argues that human frailty is a leader's strength not a weakness (Ancona et al., 2007) and that we should celebrate those leaders we might model ourselves on rather than those we worship. Furthermore, a continued adherence to the charismatic superhero indicates a failure to keep up with the literature on entrepreneurial leadership which now talks about an entrepreneurial team rather than an individual (Harper, 2008). Thus, the lone, heroic entrepreneur is an oversimplification of the reality – effective entrepreneurial leadership has moved away from the single-minded pursuit of profit with underlying drivers of certainty and predictability towards embracing the numerous opportunities for collaboration and the harnessing of good, creative and potentially risky ideas at all levels of the business in order to make the business sustainable and responsive to the needs of those who invest in it (Blundell and Lockett, 2011). Similar to transformational leadership, the entrepreneurial team is developed by a creative, reflective leader to have shared vision, goals and commitments in order to succeed, and in this manifestation entrepreneurial leadership may be a model that early years leaders might be willing to embrace (Leeson, 2014). It is certainly true that early years practitioners of all levels have been very creative at doing great things with very little.

In Chapter 1, we used building blocks as an analogy to understand modernity and post-structuralism whereby modernity was a pre-ordered construction and post-structuralism was an opportunity to dismantle the bricks and rebuild in many different ways and patterns. What we were concerned about was what was missing or had been left out, which would not be immediately obvious until the edifice was deconstructed.

When applying the same analogy to our constructions of leadership, there should be concern that what is evidently being missed or minimised is the emotional awareness and literacy of settings, the flexibility and creativity to respond to the needs of children and families in a local context. For example, More Great Childcare (DfE, 2013), with its commodification of early childhood education and care, makes it easy to take a more hegemonic view of leadership that applies business principles and loses sight of any moral imperative or ethic of care.

Conclusion

It can be seen that over the last 20 years the early years sector has had an interesting journey in seeking to develop a creative form of leadership that meets the needs of the communities it serves, as well as addressing the political and economic requirements that are expected of it. Developing from a highly feminised, low-status occupation towards a profession with clearly stated values, ethics and theoretical underpinning, however contested and debated, has required a close inspection of various leadership theories. The strong underlying belief within the sector that early years settings should not be regarded as homogenous has led to an acceptance that leaders should be similarly varied in the way they lead and that society should embrace and celebrate the differences between them. A post-structuralist view is that we should take a 'bricolage' approach (constructing something from a wide range of things that are not always associated), where leaders, immersed in leadership philosophy, are able to develop their own theory with a small 't', taking a little bit of this and a little bit of that to create an authentic style that suits their personality and strengths, as well as meeting the demands of the ever-increasing array of stakeholders and the needs of the community they seek to support (Cunha, 2005). It has been argued that adopting and enacting such a pragmatic and eclectic approach makes it possible for leaders to subvert the panoptic, regulatory gaze (see Chapter 2) that has become so all-encompassing, and for some, extremely intrusive, and this has to be attractive to creative and innovative leaders.

Continuing to use the building block analogy from Chapter 1 and earlier in this chapter, a bricolage approach would fit very well with our current ideas of individualised, highly contextualised leadership. Where no theory is totally rejected, each contributes to the mix and has potential. Indeed, it is clear from earlier in this chapter that as a new leadership theory has emerged, it has held discernible elements of earlier iterations in its pedigree. Thus, early years leaders are merely following that tradition in their quest for a leadership framework that makes sense to them individually and possibly collectively. What has been interesting is the shift in emphasis from how leaders are identified to how leaders lead and enable others to lead (Marinova et al., 2013). There is an acceptance that there may be some central issues that are important such as the capacity to create and communicate a vision that has a social justice basis; the ability to communicate; the foregrounding of relationships in everything undertaken; and the embracing of both an ethic of care and the responsibility of making decisions for the setting and the community.

Leadership (like quality) is therefore a construct that is firmly situated within community development and whilst early years leaders have embraced this, it still remains for politicians and policy makers to do so too. The shift from a modernist positivism that saw leadership as an identifiable and quantifiable object to a post-structural stance of what, why and who has shaped understandings of leadership requires that leadership is seen as the interplay between different perspectives, cultures and norms (Ladkins, 2013).

> **Reflection Point**
>
> Consider the different leadership theories that we have discussed in this chapter. Which of the styles do you identify with? Which do you find challenging to your way of thinking?

What we can conclude about leadership is that it is found in the relationship between people and most often in the little things that happen daily within a setting. It more often depends on the ability to deal with uncertainty, opposition, criticism and resistance than on abilities to influence, motivate or communicate vision (Karp and Helgo, 2008). The attempts of individual leaders to create their own leadership philosophy, techniques, tools and strategies are as varied as the settings they lead, but all have some basis in the plethora of theories explored in this chapter. It is an important characteristic of early education leaders that they are not prepared to adopt a leadership theory without comment, but are willing to investigate and explore its worth and creatively employ its more useful features in their leadership bricolage (Dunlop, 2008).

We will go on to explore the manifestations of those individual styles in the coming chapters, seeking to add to the debate and assist leaders in their personal quest for the way forward.

Chapter Summary

- It can be helpful to group the main leadership theories under headings of transactional, transformational and heroic.
- Leadership theory has significantly developed from a concentration on rigid and highly predictable traits and styles towards a more creative, individualised 'bricolage' that is highly principled and based on a recognition of the importance of relationships and an ethic of care.
- Thus, leadership is about more than managing the tasks of the setting – it's also about the complexities of relationships.
- Leadership is therefore highly contextual, negotiated and not easily transported.

Further Reading

McDowall Clark, R. and Murray, J. (2012) *Reconceptualising Leadership in the Early Years*. London: Open University Press.

Rory McDowall Clark and Janet Murray offer a new perspective on leadership that is both challenging and exciting to consider.

Moss, P. (2014) 'Early childhood policy in England 1997–2013: anatomy of a missed opportunity', *International Journal of Early Years Education*, 22 (4): 346–58.

Peter Moss gives a succinct and helpful overview of policy for early childhood that is critical in its exploration of the many opportunities for imaginative development that have been missed.

4

EARLY YEARS LEADERS – ALL THINGS TO ALL PEOPLE

Chapter Overview

Whilst we have considered the limits of Ofsted as a measure of quality and a form of technocratic control, it is symbolic of the pressure that has been brought to bear on leaders and their leadership capacity as the quest for measurable quality has dominated the early years discourse. In this chapter, we will be seeking to shed light on exactly what it is that early years leaders do and how they seek to balance the many tensions they encounter between several aspects of their role. We will also be looking at the debate on what leadership is and what management is and how the constant change of names from leader to manager creates a tension of its own for people to deal with.

Finally, in concluding the chapter, we will look forward to Part Three by raising essential questions for practice.

The Many Accountabilities of Early Years Leaders

What remains unclear, despite considerable research and debate, is how effective leadership contributes to the overall quality of the environment. Some suggest that it is the ability to build a community by holding the team together, boosting morale, maintaining and supporting effective structures, or else the ability to evaluate and plan for the future (Jones and Pound, 2008). Others argue that it is the ability to care for all members of the setting, including staff (McEldowney et al., 2009). We have already

64 LEADERSHIP

noted that the judgement of effective leadership seems to be solely based on the academic achievement of the children and measurable quality outcomes (Muijs et al., 2004), as demonstrated in the UK by the recent school readiness campaign orchestrated by the government and articulated through the Ofsted inspectorate (Ofsted, 2014) and More Great Childcare (DfE, 2013). Thus, the panoptic gaze of Ofsted and, by implication, the government, would appear to have a powerful role in dictating the focus and ethos of the work done by settings, which can have a deleterious impact on the well-being of staff, leaders and ultimately the children and families attending. By looking at the accountabilities of early years leaders, we can begin to understand the realities of that pressure and begin to construct our own understandings of quality and leadership that are sustaining and relevant.

In recognition that quality early years services are about quality experiences for children (and reflecting pedagogical thinking that positions the child at the centre of planning and provision), whilst also recognising the different stakeholders who have a perspective on quality (as outlined in Chapter 2), Figure 4.1 has been constructed to demonstrate the critical role

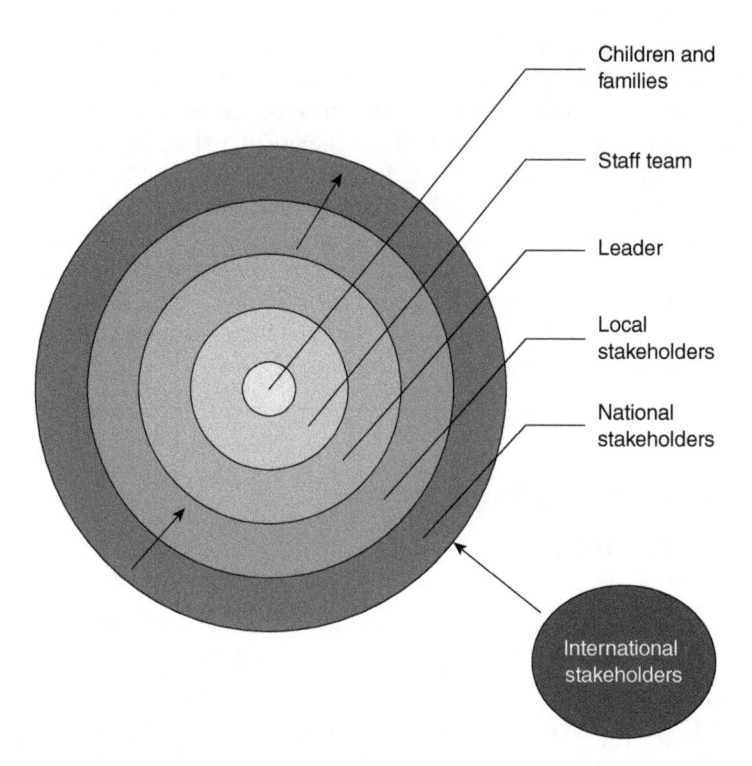

Figure 4.1 The critical role of the leader

of the leader as existing within a middle strata answerable to all layers. We conceived the leader as being all things to all people and became interested in how the concomitant expectations are navigated by each leader as they seek to address all the issues that demand their attention. We have made use of the ecological development model designed by Bronfenbrenner (1979) as a mechanism for exploring the influence of environmental factors, both within and outside the home, on a child's development. Bronfenbrenner saw his model as interactive; that whilst children are influenced by these external factors, they also influence their environment in a reciprocal process. Following the discussion in previous chapters on the strong relational discourse that is a powerful feature of early years leadership of quality, we felt it appropriate to use this framework to explore what leaders do and the interactivity they engage in on a daily basis.

The accountabilities of early years leaders

In Figure 4.1, early years leaders are deliberately positioned in the middle stratum with bottom-up responsibilities of listening to the children and families in their care (the circle in the middle of the diagram) and seeking to establish and maintain a healthy working environment for their staff (second layer in the centre). The figure draws together what we have been exploring in the previous chapters around the many demands that are placed on early years leaders from a range of stakeholders. Early years leaders are impacted on by top-down initiatives from national and local stakeholders such as the government department responsible for early years services, inspection processes and local authority Children's Services and other community bodies (positioned as the penultimate layer as they too experience the initiative and expectations of national stakeholders, especially the government). An additional pressure, represented by the separate bubble, is the developing international narrative on the leadership of quality. Whilst in Chapters 1 and 2 we explored how these various aspects have influenced quality, they also have an influence on leadership. An awareness of different early years models and leadership practices in other countries has helped to inform and shape the development of services here in the UK (Moss and Penn, 1996) and gives us pause for thought (Woodrow and Busch, 2008). Just as international perspectives on quality (considered in Chapters 1 and 2) help provide alternative ways of thinking about things, so do international perspectives on leadership. They can prevent parochialism through their offer of alternative cultural perspectives, such as the established emphasis placed on the education and training of staff in other countries and the high status of early years practitioners (Ho, 2008; Leeson et al., 2012).

Bottom-up accountabilities

Whilst in Chapters 1 and 2 we were critical of how policy can restrict understandings of quality and in Chapter 3 we expressed our concerns about one-size-fits-all approaches to leadership, not all of policy is constraining or at odds with the views of early years leaders. For example, a political interest in both quality and leadership has opened up spaces for discussing what both of these mean for the early years, but there are other policy goals that we think are aligned to the history and philosophy of early years provision, such as the focus on the needs of the child. Whilst we express our concerns that the child has become a project to be got 'right', we do feel that the ever-evolving focus on the rights of the child is important – it is the manner in which it is currently being articulated that is concerning.

The child

The child at the centre has been a cornerstone of public policy as regards improving outcomes for children, especially those who have greater need for intervention and/or support since policy initiatives began to be developed (see Hendrick, 1997). A focus on the child can be evident in some form in policy (primarily in the western world) for at least the last 100 years, if not longer. However, it has become particularly prominent in recent history in the UK. The Children Act 2004 which established the Common Assessment Framework and the legislation that accompanied the policy framework Every Child Matters (DfES, 2004), promoted a visualisation of the child at the centre – the most important entity in any decision-making and planning processes related to the family. Furthermore, the Early Years Foundation Stage (DfE, 2014) makes it explicit that children should be regarded as unique individuals and that all curriculum planning, activities and assessments should be undertaken with that perspective in mind and engage the child in the process. In Chapter 5, we look in more detail at the pedagogical roots of planning early years services around the interests of the child in order to appreciate that it is not just policy (whether in legislation or curriculum guidance) that has taken an interest in the child at the centre of early years services. The ideological position of the child as unique and at the centre of all planning and decision making is a powerful step forward in recognising the authority of the individual child (an appreciation of the child as being rather than becoming) and is not before time. In Chapter 2, we discussed the importance of social agency and there has been considerable pressure to regard the child as active and capable in terms of helping to develop learning and living opportunities (Lancaster, 2002). The autonomous child, who is an active social agent, has become a feature of both policy and practice, and whilst in Chapter 5 we explore the idea that such an approach seems logical for a service that is focused on children, here we consider how the term seems to be moving away from liberating children towards holding leaders to account.

The impact of the child at the centre on leaders is one of a powerful, explicit *accountability* which has to be recognised as fairly recent and therefore one that may not yet be fully embedded in the practice of all settings. Leaders who seek to embrace a child-oriented approach may find resistance from others (staff, parents) to their attempts to create a service that is fully bottom-up, one where the children have an active and powerful role in determining the activities and organisation of the setting. Being clear as to what the setting does to facilitate children's involvement and the authentic positioning of the child at the centre is a critical leadership function that forms part of the inspection process with Ofsted, who will scrutinise any evidence that a setting has taken the child into account in planning services and the quality of that involvement. The self-evaluation form (SEF) that should be completed before an Ofsted inspection visit asks for such evidence to be collected and demonstrated, and inspectors may wish to discuss with the children attending on the day of their visit what they think of the provision and the setting. The question of how this might happen does not seem to be addressed and many leaders may feel considerable pressure as they identify ways in which they might gather such information – ways that are appropriate and meaningful rather than superficial and tokenistic. We have observed settings having text boxes on their paperwork that the child is encouraged to draw in or where they are to choose a smiley or grumpy face to indicate their feelings and we question the meaningfulness of this process for the child or the setting. We would suggest that leaders explore the potential of the Mosaic Approach, developed by Clark and Moss (2011), which demonstrates effective co-construction strategies where the emphasis is on listening to children – a crucial aspect of developing responsive and reciprocal relationships within a setting. It is a positive development that the importance of child engagement is formally recognised. However, it is concerning that this formalisation of good practice into something that is measurable can result in a greater focus on the scrutiny process than on the empowering and engaging of children. It creates a form of technocratic control and shifts the principle of empowerment from a value base to something that has to be systematically measured rather than being omnipresent and part of the fabric of the setting's culture and ethos. Leaders therefore become fixated on how they might evidence their practice, establishing charts and other protocols rather than allowing relationships to develop in a natural, mutually respectful manner. What we noted in Chapter 2 is that where distributed leadership occurs, it would appear that settings are better at involving children in ways that are naturalistic, helpful and meaningful, forging a link between the quality of the setting, the principle of valuing the autonomous child and leadership styles.

The family

We also positioned the child's family as central to the process of the role of a leader – a position that might be regarded as self-evident as parents are the ones to select and engage the services of a setting. However, this positioning can cause considerable tension as parents are increasingly encouraged to regard themselves as powerful purchasers and consumers when considering their choice of childcare services (see Chapter 2). To further this capacity, parents have been given mechanisms such as formal complaint procedures, access to Ofsted inspections and materials, in order to hold settings to account for the services they offer. Almost as an unintended consequence of the parent's charter introduced by the government in 1991 which emphasised the rights of parents to make choices and demands on the services they wished to engage, parents have been encouraged to feel powerful in making demands of services they are paying for and to use the ultimate sanction of removing their child if they remain unhappy. At first glance, none of that would seem complicated or undesirable; of course there should be a high level of accountability and a sense of shared care between settings and families, but we discern a creeping consumerism that is exemplified in the development of a mixed economy of care where private business is encouraged to become engaged in the provision of services, which has promoted a commodification of services viewed by some as unhealthy and unhelpful to the creation of good partnerships (Penn, 2011a). Given that in Chapter 2 we explored how parents are not always accurate judges of quality, the development of an ideology of early years services as a marketplace could be problematic, particularly where the market may be limited in what it offers.

There are a number of projects that look at the development of good relationships with families (Boag-Munroe, 2014) and many government initiatives that have sought to promote partnerships between settings and families. This is a relatively new phenomenon that may have become important as we increase the professionalisation of what used to be a community-responsive resource and thereby created barriers between the different stakeholders. The emphasis on working in partnership with parents may also be more to do with the deficit model discussed in Chapter 3 and a method of compensating for their perceived inadequacies, both in terms of their parenting skills and their limitations in understanding and providing for their children's needs. The literature on working in partnership suggests that particular skills and initiatives are needed in terms of accessibility, engagement and frequent communication strategies such as parents' evenings, open days, key working and communication books (Campbell, 2011; Royston and Rodrigues, 2013). Issues of power and equality are key for leaders to consider in all their actions; communicating a system of full involvement in a child's life can be complex and is often open to misinterpretation and misunderstanding. Furthermore, a policy of promoting parental engagement is founded on an assumption that all parents wish to be involved at equal levels, whereas many do not for a variety of reasons and we explore the implications of this in Chapter 6. Parents who do not wish to engage are often negatively positioned as 'hard to reach' which is erroneous and an unhelpful label to attach to people, creating a further barrier to the development of effective relationships between settings and families. Leaders therefore have to navigate a very careful course with individual families, determining the level of communication the family require/wish and marrying that with local and national expectations about engagement with those regarded as vulnerable (another value-laden and socially constructed term that may shift with time and competing ideologies). Thus, leaders and their staff may find themselves in a state of tension as they manage the differing expectations of the families that use their services – a tension that needs diplomacy and clarity of policy, aims and objectives as well as a well-communicated mission statement or vision.

The team

Accountability to the staff team is a further bottom-up aspect that leaders have to observe. As discussed in Chapter 3, a number of leadership models have been developed and adopted that regard the relationship between a leader and his/her staff team as critical to the well-being of the setting, with the leader facilitating the ability of individual staff members to take on responsibility (i.e. distributed leadership) and reach their own potential (i.e. transformational leadership). This can be problematic; leaders all too often struggle to relinquish power and/or authority, often regarding themselves as the sole unit of power in the setting and thereby holding all responsibility and accountability. They may also find it difficult to find staff members who are prepared to take on responsibility, preferring instead to be led rather than participate in leading. McDowall Clark and Murray (2012) suggest that the development of an inner core of passionate care (moral purpose plus ethic of care) will assist with creating and supporting effective bottom-up accountability. For them, this inner, strongly driven and principled desire that leaders should do well for the children, families and staff they are responsible for (as discussed in Chapter 2), helps to create the energy needed to make a positive contribution to the development of effective early years services. Leaders should, therefore, feel 'constructive discontent' (McDowall Clark and Murray, 2012: 47) that urges leaders to do the best they can and not accept poor quality in the work of the setting, challenging staff to aspire to higher principles and to commit to the leader's vision of the setting's aims and objectives.

Of course, team members also have a responsibility to make the setting the best it can be and there has been an active dialogue as to the accountability of followers (Baker, 2007; Kupers, 2007). Followers are no longer perceived as unthinking and passive; instead, they are expected to be active and participative in the decision-making processes and actions of the setting. The responsibility of the leader is to create a permissive environment that communicates the sense of value they hold for their team, thereby enabling a 'relational interdependence' (McDowall Clark and Murray, 2012: 71) to occur. This enabling process demands a lot of time and energy as well as a willingness to relinquish some control and stop acting in automatic, top-down authoritative modes that may be more familiar to the leader or seen as more productive in the short term: getting the job done being more important than the discursive process that a more democratic model would advocate. So, leaders have to actively seek an egalitarian, accessible style of leadership that promotes a respectful environment that enables effective bottom-up mechanisms for action. This can be tough, especially when seen in the context of top-down narratives and expectations that also impact on leaders, positioned as they are in that middle layer. Once again, we identify a shift from modernist, directive principles towards a post-structuralist model of dialogue and co-construction happening at a very local level to achieve the best for that community. As we will discuss in more detail in Chapters 5 and 6, the process of working as a team to consider understandings of quality and how best to realise them can facilitate the process of deconstructing top-down accountability models and appreciating where there are gaps and space for interpretation and innovation in what is being asked of early years practice.

Top-down accountabilities

We have already explored in depth in Chapters 1 and 2 the pressures from top-down accountability – the need to demonstrate that the early years 'works' and achieves the desired outcomes. We have framed these accountability structures in relation to the global and the national. In particular, in regard to the national we have talk about the panoptic gaze and how it seeks to monitor and control early years leadership. However, there are many levels to the accountability structures. Serious impacts on the thoughts, actions and energy levels of a leader are also made by the top-down expectations and directives of the local community, including the local authority, as well as any other agencies with which the setting works closely such as Children's Services, Health Visiting and the police authority. Many settings have a management committee made up of parents and other local stakeholders who seek to hold the leader to account at regular meetings where the curriculum, finances and other aspects of management are closely inspected by members. Management committees frequently change membership – usually at annual general meetings (AGM), where leaders often find themselves in the position of regularly revisiting old arguments and debates as someone new enters the scene and asks questions that have already been addressed.

Local Authority Children's Services departments are charged under the Children Act 2004 with developing a plan for the provision of services for all children and families in their catchment area. These plans will very likely include expectations for early years provision and the development of services for key groups. For example, government objectives in the UK for local authorities regarding the provision of services to children aged 2 years; the detection of children at risk of abuse, especially sexual exploitation; and increased awareness of/responsiveness to 'vulnerable' families, have all placed a high level of expectation on leaders to respond, develop services and take account of the varying needs of their community. The provision of early education places for disadvantaged children aged 2 years has been implemented in the UK as a strategy for improving the prospects of children from an impoverished background and has required considerable thought and preparation to be effective and responsive. At the outset of the allocation of funding for providing early education places for 2-year-olds, it was identified that not all settings have expertise in working with children aged 2, so staff development and appropriate curriculum planning have been the main focus for many (Georgeson et al., 2014). Working within a context of prioritisation of services for subsections of the population demands a shift away from an ideology of universal services and may cause difficulties for settings firmly embedded in the local landscape when they have to explain to families that their services are now restricted. There are also considerable contextual expectations on settings; rural settings may well be charged with looking at how they might offer services to a widespread community with little or no access to transport and urban settings may have to deal with other forms of deprivation. Thus, the expectation of local authorities to secure sufficient early years provision becomes a top-down pressure for the early years leader who is expected to respond positively to the demands of national policy.

We have already outlined in Chapter 2 how national inspection systems such as Ofsted become a part of the process of monitoring early years providers in how they implement policy. Nationally, leaders of settings are expected to fulfil the legal requirements of their registration and to submit themselves to regular inspection and self-evaluation systems. Whilst earlier we explored the idea that inspection acts as a mechanism for monitoring the setting, there is also the view that it is about monitoring the effectiveness of the leadership. Leadership of the setting is a major component of the Ofsted inspection, with leaders being asked to provide evidence of their leadership of the EYFS, leadership of their staff, their safeguarding responsibilities and their partnerships with parents and external agencies (Ofsted, 2014). As already indicated, leaders are expected to engage in a self-evaluation process that is also closely scrutinised as inspectors decide on the grade they plan to give the setting. The grading has a key role in the future success or longevity of the setting, as well as determining whether a setting continues to get funding to offer things such as the early years education entitlement, and also how parents (as consumers) perceive the setting. Whilst steps have been taken to remedy concerns that inspectors are too education oriented (Spencer and Dubiel, 2013), there remains a further criticism that the inspection process requires settings to be sufficiently similar in nature in order for comparisons to be made, meaning that important contextual and cultural aspects of the setting (such as responding to the needs and interests of children and their families) may be lost.

A further layer of complexity is the responsibility that leaders have to develop the workforce in line with government targets. Each setting is expected to have at least 50 per cent of the workforce qualified at level 3 or above and to demonstrate the continuing professional development of the staff group as a whole. There is much debate about the qualifications available to early years practitioners and whether they are robust and fit for purpose (Nutbrown, 2012), but these concerns sit outside of the complexities we noted in Chapter 2 regarding what is a good member of staff and the role of dispositions and attitudes. Targets around qualification levels reflect the modernist agendas that we discussed in Chapter 1 – easy-to-quantify features of quality. However, such a quantitative exercise does little to say what qualifications should look like or what it is that they should do. Staff development is therefore both a bottom-up and a top-down level of accountability and is muddled by constant debate and change.

However, managing the educational ambitions of the staff team whilst maintaining the ratios and workload of the setting and keeping the vision of development and aspiration are made more difficult by the amalgamation of the Graduate Leader Fund, a ring-fenced pot for the training of early years workers, into the early intervention budgets of the local authority. The Graduate Leader Fund was intended to support the government commitment to have a graduate leader in every setting by 2015 and seemed to be fulfilling the objective of improving the quality of settings in terms of their leadership, staff development and overall capacity for creative and responsive practice (Mathers et al., 2011). A less charitable view might be that the fund was designed to upskill leaders in a particular direction – towards being an entrepreneurial manager that achieves a pre-determined set of outcomes laid down by policy makers and externally assessed. Nevertheless, the subsuming of this money has meant that financial resources to support professional development are much harder to come by, so many settings do what they have to and no more as they are unable to afford any more than that. It should also be noted that the NPQICL programme, an exclusive learning opportunity for early years leaders, has been ring-fenced for children's centre leaders only and has moved from its original egalitarian, leadership framework to a training perspective with a strong emphasis on outcomes and 'narrowing the gap' deficit model strategies. Removal of access to effective funding mechanisms or inspiring leadership education programmes might also be seen as a disruption of the contract between services and the authorities and therefore lead to frustration and low morale.

A leader is therefore required to make decisions on a daily basis that manage and balance the competing claims on their time and energy. A modernist view of the leadership of quality settings that appears to focus on a managerialist stance where balancing books and showing great leaps in children's developmental progression are privileged, creates a phenomenal pressure that only highly creative and resilient leaders are able to resist. Decisions are made constantly as to what constitutes a list of priorities and which of many, often competing, priorities is the best one for immediate focus and how all of the demands being made fit with the ethics, values and principles of the setting, the staff and the leader themselves. The ability to wear many different hats, often at the same time and always with an apparently seamless transition, is key to successful leadership, which demands a great deal of the leader's skills and abilities, confidence and knowledge. It has been suggested that the principles of authentic leadership – leaders being authentic and true to themselves; having self-awareness, relational transparency, balanced processing and an internalised moral perspective – are regarded as best placed to help leaders with this juggling act (Avolio and Gardner, 2005; Begley, 2001; Champy, 2009) and assist in creating high-quality, responsive and creative environments for young children to inhabit.

We have identified a further pressure which is that exerted by international stakeholders and Chapter 1 discussed the activities of organisations such as the World Bank, the OECD, Unicef and the EU and their impact on the development of quality frameworks and expectations of early years settings in providing the learning foundations for a future workforce. The work of these organisations has a further impact on the leadership of early years settings, setting out expectations around qualifications, structures and ethos for leaders to meet and comply with. There is a substantial literature relating to early years leadership in other countries and a number of high-level discussions have taken place in recent times as to how that work impacts on service provision, leadership and qualifications in this country – we refer you to the discussion on the role of the pedagogue in Europe that informed decision making around Early Years Professional Status (EYPS; CWDC, 2006).

Internal accountability: the emotional labour of leading an early years setting

It can be concluded that leaders of early years settings balance a substantial number of tensions and navigate their way through many difficult and emotionally demanding situations. An emerging story has been the recognition of the significant emotional work that is present in people industries such as early years, education and welfare. Originally defined as a sociological concept observed in the work done by flight attendants (Hochschild, 1983), the concept has been acknowledged as present in any work that involves activities with other people – nursing, social work (Mann, 2004), teaching and, most recently, early years (Elfer and Dearnley, 2007). Emotional labour is defined as the amount of effort that is involved in work that requires the production of an emotional state in another person: 'The emotional style of offering the service is part of the service itself' (Hochschild, 1983: 5). In early years work, meeting the needs of the child is often seen as an emotional response reflecting the ethic of care that should be a strong guiding principle (see Chapter 2).

Emotional labour is also present where employers seek to control the emotional activities of their employees by being explicit as to the actions and reactions that are acceptable to the organisation. **Emotionology**, the societal view of what constitutes an acceptable display of emotion (Crawford, 2014), adds a further layer of control that has to be navigated and negotiated. A good example is the restrictions, on the grounds of safeguarding, that might be placed on the actions of staff when required to console a distressed child, such as a recommendation to place a cushion on your lap when comforting a child to avoid any close and intimate contact. Thus, early years work requires a high degree of emotional engagement and has substantial emotional labour costs (Elfer and Dearnley, 2007) that are not always fully appreciated by all stakeholders. Emotional labour requires workers to manage their feelings in accordance with the feeling rules of the organisation they work for, by either suppressing those emotions that are deemed undesirable or by inducing those which are expected. This is achieved either through surface acting – pretending the emotions that are expected – or deep acting where a worker draws on deeper, personal reserves of emotion to bring forth the required emotional display (Hochschild, 1983). Children are able to discern when the adult caring for them is 'going through the motions' and will react accordingly, often by dismissing the adult as uncaring and incapable of creating a sustainable and nourishing relationship (Leeson, 2009), which is at odds with what the worker wants to achieve. Thus, the effort involved can be substantial, especially when the rules are at odds with personal values and beliefs (Syed, 2008) or where there is limited support or recognition of the hard work engaged in (Smith, 1992). In such instances, workers either become exhausted trying to balance the pressures or they resolve the tension by distancing themselves from the emotional impact of their work, becoming blasé, remote or disengaged as a result (Mann, 2004).

For early years work, recognition of the impact of emotional labour is really important given how far it has moved away from its heritage as a female occupation supporting other women with childcare responsibilities. A gendered discourse of women as natural carers of young children has been and remains powerful in many countries. However, this is not to suggest we believe that women have a monopoly on the ability to care for young children – far from it, as there should be increased efforts to promote the involvement of men in the care of young children. There are concerns that a shift towards more entrepreneurial approaches to leadership could be seen as an attempt to limit an ethic of care and introduce business attributes more traditionally associated with males (Osgood, 2006), but the debates on understandings of gender are complex and extend far beyond the scope of this book. Our concern is that regarding emotional labour in gendered terms can potentially exclude men from the early years workforce, but also runs the risk of exploiting women's presumed caring capacity (Georgeson and Campbell-Barr, 2015). However, a shift towards more business-like principles also provides a fertile space for the development of expectations that workers will engage in surface acting rather than deep acting, feeling their work and having a strong commitment to it. The role of emotions in early years work highlights the complex discursive structures that surround working with children, such as understandings of gender and child protection alongside models of effective leadership. The contradiction is that early years work is now positioned as more than 'just' care; it is complex and multi-faceted (Harwood et al., 2013), meaning that the emotional aspects of the work should be regarded as extremely important and yet they seem to have become subordinate to other pressures.

It should be considered that leaders of early years settings are especially vulnerable to burnout or disengagement as there is little opportunity for them to gain support for their role; very few have an effective professional support network, relying instead on family and friends who are not always the best or most appropriate people to help. A leader is not likely to talk openly and honestly about their concerns and difficulties with other leaders in their local area as they are technically business rivals. It would also be inappropriate to talk to their staff in such detail, so establishing strong, reliable and effective support mechanisms is very important, yet frequently overlooked or disregarded. Support for new leaders is also very important. Many leaders emerge from the existing staff team and are unlikely to have had training for their role beforehand. Somehow they are expected to 'become' a leader almost overnight and with limited resources or reference points. There has been a development towards leaders finding mentors for themselves or making links with colleagues from afar to enable those necessary conversations to take place without anxiety as to market position or any conflicts of interest occurring. These have proved nourishing and beneficial and should be actively promoted. Neglecting your own support needs as a leader renders your leadership potentially unsustainable; it's not an indulgence.

The Many Titles of Early Years Leaders

The increased engagement in theoretical debates as to how we construct understandings of leadership, as explored in Chapter 3, creates a further set of external pressures for leaders to negotiate. In particular, there has been a plethora of titles ascribed to the person deemed to be responsible or in charge and there is a discernible historical pattern to the choice of titles which reflects the culture of the time. Equally, many of these names have been used interchangeably and indiscriminately which contributes to a lack of clarity and hence confusion as to what the expectations are which might be placed on those who perform that role. To begin with, leaders of voluntary or community early years settings were most commonly called pre-school or playgroup supervisors – a very practical title with connotations of an organiser who took responsibility for the day-to-day functions of the setting, ensuring a smooth, predictable and reliable basic operation. Settings provided by the local authority, such as nursery schools or classes, had a head (mistress/master) in charge, giving a clear message of the professional authority that existed within a recognisable education-based framework. More latterly, we have seen the emergence of terms such as 'leader', 'manager' and 'chief executive'. Many documents seem to use the terms interchangeably (for example, Ofsted, 2014), which suggests that there exists a mindset that sees acompatibility between the terms that allows them to mean similar things. Qualifications have also been used as a way of noting different levels of expertise and responsibility within an organisation – Early Years Professional (EYP) and now Early Years Teacher (EYT). The lack of an agreed, consistent title for those who are responsible for the delivery of services to children and families calls into question the authority and power attached to the role and causes confusion amongst those who are involved, not least the leader/manager/head/supervisor/chief executive/owner themselves.

Within the early years care and education sector, we have seen the development of 'leader' as the preferred title over the last few years and there have been many writers promoting the concept of leadership (Aubrey, 2007; Leeson, 2010; Murray and McDowall Clark, 2013; Rodd, 2006). Hall (1996) debated the common (mis)perception that management is a masculine term and, thus, may have fallen into disfavour as more women entered the senior levels of organisations (in her case, schools). Her conclusion, and that of others (Murray and McDowall Clark, 2013), is that the male/female dichotomy is a false one (as we begin to suggest above). Pedler et al. (2004) suggest that we should not be surprised at the emergence of leadership as a preferred descriptor of the person at the top; for them, it arises from the recognition of the complexity of modern organisations. They suggest that in earlier times the owner of a company had a leadership role, in developing the business and creating new opportunities whilst the manager ensured the maintenance of the workforce. Increased distance between owners and the workforce in a modern context means that there is a requirement for the embodiment of the leadership that owners previously held and that managers are not equipped to do. In an early years context, we have seen an increase in the involvement of large national organisations creating and developing substantial local and national chains of nurseries and childminders. Interestingly (or worryingly, depending on your perspective), as a consequence of the financial downturn, we have also seen the development of the 'virtual leader' where a group of settings, most notably children's centres, create themselves into a cluster with one leader leading many settings and leaving the day-to-day 'management' of individual settings to lesser qualified members of staff (Bertram and Pascal, 2014), so once again we are beginning to see the re-emergence of the 'manager' as a key person within the setting.

The lack of a consistent title leads to concern and confusion as to what it is that this person does – do they lead or do they manage? In turn, this level of confusion takes us to a more global debate as to what is leadership and what is management – are they the same or different and are the tasks done by the same person or by different people? Further questions arise as to whether leadership and management should co-exist, or might one be forgotten within an organisation in preference for the other, and if so, which should that be? There are many voices in this debate, mostly advocating the loss of ritual and unimaginative management tasks and roles in favour of more creative, emotionally literate leadership responsibilities (Owen, 2000). Management has been characterised as being rationalist-scientific with a bureaucratic approach to tasks and a focus on outcomes and production procedures, whereas leadership could be viewed as a more creative focus on the process and the well-being of staff and children (McDowall Clark and Murray, 2012). These different ideological positions are also highlighted by Solly (2003) who describes management as maintenance and leadership as development.

It may be (and certainly the literature would suggest this is the case) that being a leader is more creative and exciting than being a very staid, careful and predictable manager, but Hall (1996: 11) argues that leadership and management are so integral to each other that: 'Managing without leadership [is] unethical: leadership without management [is] irresponsible', meaning that there are essential elements of both that should exist together, either being embodied in one person or being shared with at least one other so that essential ethical dialogues can take place and decisions have firm foundations. Our research with early years leaders has shown that there are substantial risks that leadership aspects often get squeezed out as management responsibilities demand more focus and time.

Figure 4.2 seeks to identify what might be classed as management tasks, taking the definition of a manager as being more task-oriented (procedure led) and a leader being more people oriented (process led) (Law and Glover, 2000; Owen, 2000). What we found is that there are what we would classify as procedural tasks such as paying the bills and ordering supplies (absolutely vital – one of us was once in charge of a

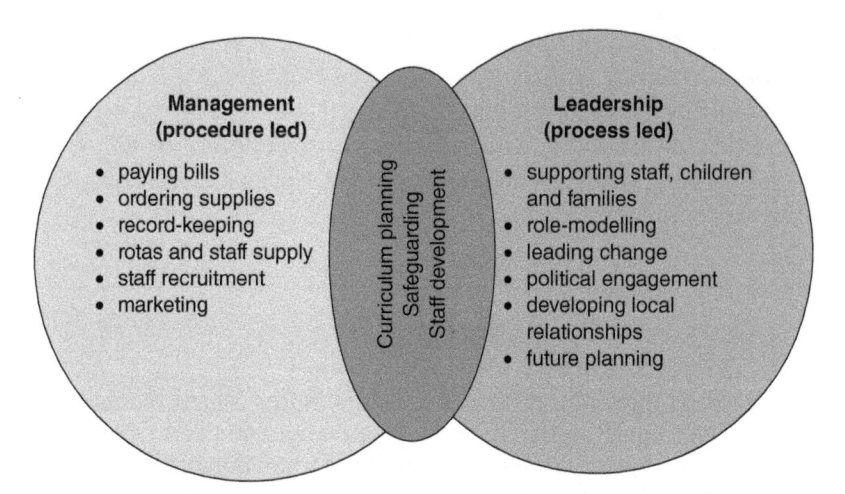

Management (procedure led)
- paying bills
- ordering supplies
- record-keeping
- rotas and staff supply
- staff recruitment
- marketing

Curriculum planning
Safeguarding
Staff development

Leadership (process led)
- supporting staff, children and families
- role-modelling
- leading change
- political engagement
- developing local relationships
- future planning

Figure 4.2 Management (procedure led) and leadership (process led) tasks within an early years setting

family centre and forgot to order any toilet rolls, which was a significant oversight at the time!) and process tasks such as supporting staff, children and families. However, there are tasks that we would argue fit across the divide and might be considered the responsibility of either the leader or the manager. Furthermore, there are tasks that might be judged as management and yet have leadership implications. For example, the management task of drawing up a staff rota may have a serious impact on the leadership responsibility to support individual members of staff in terms of their life/work balance and developmental aspirations. Thus, we are inclined to agree with the perspective put forward by Garvey and Lancaster (2010) that seeking to separate leadership and management is another unhelpful dichotomy. Instead, we should focus on their relationship and how they are held in balance by the individual responsible for an early years setting.

Thus, rather than looking at which matters more than the other, we can focus on the social construction and contextual nature of leadership with the conferment of roles and responsibilities within that dialogic process being axiomatic in identifying what people do and how they do it. In returning to post-structuralist approaches, the process of considering understandings of leadership and management is actually about contextualising these terms in relation to the discussions that have taken place previously in the chapter in order to discern who and what has shaped the definitions. Clearly, policy plays a role in constructions of leadership and management, but so too do the historical development of early years leadership, the debates on what leadership is, and also how others – parents and colleagues – position us, as leaders. Old terminology and perceived definitions die hard when new ones evolve, so it becomes about a need to engage in deconstruction and seek the right term to describe and define who it is that is responsible for the setting in regard to the context.

> **Reflection Point**
>
> You may like to think about how your setting addresses its management responsibilities whilst at the same time being dynamic and creative. You may well be attracted to aspects of distributed leadership, discussed in Chapter 3, or to being creative with your time by looking at your list of priorities and questioning their importance or relevance.

The Many Jobs of Early Years Leaders

In Figure 4.2, we made an attempt to begin to identify what those in charge of a setting do during their day. The list is not exhaustive – the work that we have done with leaders of settings (see Part Three) has highlighted and enumerated the substantial number of hats that are worn throughout the working day and the pressure experienced when moving seamlessly from one task to another – from a mundane straightforward task such as ordering supplies to a more complex task such as representing the setting at a local meeting about local authority budgets or planning an individual care or education plan for a child with special needs. The capacity to meet these demands requires a great deal of the individual and is not the only story, as we have already seen in this chapter.

The Activist Leader

As with our discussion on quality, we consider in this chapter how leadership is constructed through many different lenses and that there can often be competing demands. Yet, as with quality, it is about recognising who has constructed the knowledge around leadership and why – what are the aims and objectives? Again, post-structuralism encourages a deconstruction of the prevailing knowledge on leadership, but we believe that messages around leadership extend beyond just individual leaders. Post-structural approaches encourage a co-construction and we think that this is important for developing understandings of leadership and quality in the early years – they should be constructed with early years providers, not for them. Dahlberg and Moss (2005) discuss ethical practice in regard to not just following rules, but rather making contextualised decisions. Leadership is therefore not about performativity, it is about being relevant. We have explored in this chapter and the previous one the importance of collaboration in leadership. In Chapter 2, we referred to the 100 languages on quality in the early years; here, it is about recognising that there are 100 voices to engage with in developing a collaborative understanding of leading quality.

In Figure 4.1, we identified the relevance of international stakeholders to the development of the research and practice of other countries and settings in terms of their impact on our own development and avoiding the perils of parochialism with the concomitant risk of 'doing what we have always done'. A number of writers (Rodd, 1998; Woodrow and Busch, 2008) suggest that leaders have a responsibility to develop their role as an 'activist professional' (Woodrow and Busch, 2008: 90), taking a full part in research projects looking at the development of early years settings and engaging in public debate on important issues relating to their work. Creating learning communities locally, nationally and internationally that take the opportunity to debate recent policy changes and other developments, as well as utilising resources such as research funding, research partnerships and reflective practice, creates the dialogic space to define their practice, assert their vision, ethics and identity and gain strength from the nurturing critical relationships that are formed through this process. Positioning themselves as professional activists, early years leaders have the chance to be creative – an opportunity that might not be present in other facets of their role. To capture this creativity, a number of websites have been developed where leaders can share their stories and facilitate debate (see, for example, www.nationalcollege.org.uk/ and www.ofsted.gov.uk/).

In Part Three, we explore the work of a community of practice where leaders were invited to share their experiences and thoughts on the leadership of quality, and we highlight and debate the development of the new understandings that ensued. Throughout Part Three, we draw on the debates presented in this chapter and others in order to explore the realities of leading quality early years practice.

Chapter Summary

- The role of the leader is central in balancing the tensions and contradictions between top-down and bottom-up accountabilities.
- The tricky nature of balancing all the jobs and roles that early years leaders are expected to perform should be borne in mind.
- The division between leadership and management is a false one. Increasingly, many tasks cannot be safely defined as one or the other.
- The importance of an ethic of care underpinning the development of settings cannot be underestimated.
- It is imperative that there is recognition of the emotional labour involved in early years leadership and that resources are sought to support the role of leader.
- There is creativity and challenge involved in being a professional activist.

Further Reading

Osgood, J. (2012) *Narratives from the Nursery: Negotiating the Professional Identities in Early Childhood*. London: Routledge.
Jayne Osgood offers an excellent exploration of what it means to be a professional working in the early years sector, arguing that professionalism is a very personal issue.

Taggart, G. (2011) 'Don't we care? The ethics and emotional labour of early years professionalism', *Early Years: An International Research Journal*, 31 (1): 85–95.
Geoff Taggart argues the case for the inclusion of early years practitioners in the 'caring professions'.

PART THREE
IMPLICATIONS FOR PRACTICE

In previous chapters, we have sought to trace understandings of quality and leadership in the early years. We have considered how there are different stakeholders who are all involved in shaping the way in which quality and leadership are discussed and understood. In particular, we have highlighted the importance of recognising your own understanding of quality and leadership, and also of appreciating where these understandings have come from. We have talked about post-structuralist approaches as they attempt to deconstruct the understandings that people have about quality and leadership and to start to piece together what and who is shaping early years practice.

However, in deconstructing understandings of quality and leadership, one of the challenges is deciphering what this actually means for early years practice. One of the criticisms of deconstructing is what is left at the end – if all of the building blocks are knocked down, what does this leave to guide early years pedagogy? Equally, we have been critical of different understandings of quality and leadership, but critiquing can also leave a sense of being unsure of what is left to guide practice. We do not want to leave readers with unanswered questions, but we must also confess that we do not have all the answers. What we do in Part Three is explore the views and experiences of four early years practitioners to begin to consider what our earlier discussions mean for practice. We consider how our case study practitioners understand quality (Chapter 5) and the role of reflective practice (Chapter 6) in leading quality early years practice. In exploring the experiences of the four case study practitioners, we aim to relate back to the discussions that we have had in earlier chapters; we consider what it is that might be influencing their understandings of quality and leadership to identify how both international and local ideas shape early childhood practice. Exploring where there are international influences on early years practice enables us to discuss how the discourses present in international discussions on early years provision are not all bad. There are some discourses on early years provision that feel right for the four practitioners – all we are looking to consider is where knowledge on early years practice has come from. Readers will also notice that for the early years practitioners there is a process of making sense of their practice that is ongoing. Part of this ongoing process of sense making is the influence of the local and changing dynamics of who they work with (both adults and children). A second aspect of the sense-making process is that of reflective practice, which we consider in detail in Chapter 6.

Our Practitioners

We have an existing relationship with all of the case study practitioners. These relationships are formed around our role in delivering various forms of professional development for them, either in the form of training days or in delivering masters-level teaching (and assessment). In some instances, they have also participated in research that we have undertaken. We do not present the case study practitioners as being representative, rather we have selected them as we think they have all had interesting experiences working in the early years and also because we have enjoyed having rich and engaging discussions with them about quality and leadership in the early years. We feel that they are very honest and open in their discussions of their practice. We could have selected a different group of practitioners who may have presented different accounts of quality and leadership, so what we present in the following chapters is designed to support you in your own thinking about quality and leadership in the early years.

All four practitioners are based in the south-west of England and whilst they cover different local authorities their experiences are very much shaped by their local communities (as we will see in the following chapters). Their geographical location might also have wider implications. For example, in Chapters 1 and 2, we talked about concepts of childhood and the influence of local cultures. It is highly likely that the concepts and cultures of those in the south-west are different to those in London or Newcastle. The decision to live in the south-west might also have an influence on how the practitioners understand a 'good' childhood. We do not want to dismiss these influences, but ask you, the reader, to be mindful of them as you read the case studies.

Jacky

Jacky is a childminder who delivers early education 'pre-school' sessions for children aged 2–4 years. She started her career in early education and childcare seven years ago, attracted into the sector by the Early Years Professional Status (EYPS). She has always practised as a registered childminder, but in the last four years she has focused exclusively on the delivery of early education sessions.

Sue

Sue is the manager of a small inner-city pre-school operating out of a church hall, which she joined in September 2014. She has worked in the early years for 18 years, but not just as a manager. She also worked for a few years as a cluster group leader for a local authority and as an associate lecturer for the Open University on one of their early childhood modules.

Sandra

Sandra is the leader of a voluntary sector setting, which is a registered charity in an area of socio-economic disadvantage. It is a 'put away' setting based in a church hall. The setting takes children from the age of 2 years to 5 years, but does not separate the children by age. Sandra has been employed at the setting since 1999; prior to that, in 1995, she was the chair of a pre-school committee, a parent volunteer and then a student. In her previous career, she worked for the Ministry of Defence, the Navy and the RAF, which has helped with her understanding of the management and leadership role and also the business side of the setting.

Cheryl

Cheryl runs a volunteers-based pre-school playgroup (with 20 children attending at any one time) that is a registered charity, and which she has been with for 27 years. The ethos of the setting is to be inclusive in its provision for the children and families who choose to come there. Its aim is to provide a welcoming, stimulating and caring environment where children can learn and develop at their own individual rate through making choices and assessing risk benefits.

The Writing Framework

We asked the four practitioners to come together and consider their understandings of quality and how they look to lead quality early years practice. Each of them was asked to come prepared to talk about both quality and leadership, having been provided with the following questions to act as prompts (though not as an exhaustive guide) for their thinking:

1. What is their understanding of quality and what has shaped and/or influenced that understanding?
2. What are their thoughts on quality inspection frameworks and staff qualifications and any challenges that have arisen in the effort to lead quality?
3. How do they lead good quality provision and what are the implications (compromises and challenges) for the setting and their leadership?
4. How do they deal with the requirement to negotiate between top-down policy definitions of quality and the bottom-up perspectives of the parents and children who access the setting?

It is important to acknowledge that these questions have been shaped by our experiences of writing this book and of drawing together debates on quality and leadership in the early years. The areas that we identified have clearly been shaped by what we have presented in earlier chapters and it is something of a conundrum as to whether we have created a particular discourse (a way of thinking and speaking about) early years practice. Whilst we expressed to the four practitioners that they were free in their writing, we have to be mindful that both we and them are subject to discursive processes, so there are limits as to how free any writing can be. What we tried to do is ask questions of what they wrote, first through them asking questions of each other, and second, in us writing around their experiences. To facilitate the former of these, we asked the practitioners to share their ideas with each other via a (sort of) speed-dating exercise. When speaking to each other, they were encouraged to ask questions and note down anything that felt pertinent to them. We then talked to them as a group about what they had written down. We also asked each of them to go away and write approximately 500 words on quality and 500 words on leading quality early years provision, based on their initial thoughts and the subsequent discussions that had taken place. In asking them to write about leadership, we wanted them to think about the different ways that they might reflect on themselves as leaders working through a challenge that they have faced in their setting. All of the practitioners are very reflective in their approach and their previous involvement with us had involved them reflecting on their practice in various forms (e.g. essays, group discussions, action research). However, to support this reflective process, we provided examples of approaches to reflection and emphasised that they did not have to feel restricted to the written word in developing their reflections. What we have presented is their words, regarding both quality and leadership and their reflections on this. We have then written around what they said to relate back to earlier chapters.

VISIONS OF QUALITY

Chapter Overview

In this chapter, we look at how our four practitioners understand quality and relate it to earlier discussions in Chapters 1 and 2 by considering how their views reflect wider understandings of quality, but also how they are active in constructing an understanding of quality that is right for their settings. In the examples, we consider the importance of being proud of your vision of quality, enabling children to have ownership of structural features of quality, responding to the local community and adhering to Ofsted requirements. We consider the importance of recognising your principles and those of your team in developing your vision of quality, whilst being mindful of what has shaped and informed those principles.

As we outlined in the introduction to this part of the book, we present the words of the case study practitioners to illustrate some of the challenges that can be encountered when developing quality in the early years. We stress that their examples are just that – examples. These are the aspects of quality that the four practitioners chose to write about; another group may have selected different features of quality. The examples are not designed to be comprehensive of how our practitioners understand and enact quality. Given the time, each of our practitioners could write much more on how they view quality – these are just aspects that felt important to them at the time of writing. The absence of quality features, noted earlier in the book, does not mean that they are unimportant. Equally, the four practitioners found a lot of commonality in what they were saying when they met, but they were not able to write about all aspects of quality. It is likely that the ideas below will be important to many early years practitioners and leaders, but there will be many other features as well; we just consider these examples as ways of approaching your understanding of quality early years practice.

Your Vision of Quality

In previous chapters, we have emphasised the importance of *you* in developing understandings of quality and leadership – we have been asking *you* to consider what both of these terms mean for *you*. However, we are not naive in trying to emphasise your role in developing the quality of your early years setting, as we recognise that you also have to adhere to registration and legal requirements, as well as the views and expectations of other stakeholders (e.g. parents and local authority advisors), as discussed in detail in Chapters 2 and 4. In each of the examples that we have, there is an element of having to consider the views of other stakeholders: parents, Ofsted, colleagues; and we will discuss each of these. In exploring the influence of stakeholders, we discuss themes that we have raised earlier in the book, such as being mindful of where knowledge has come from (curriculum guidance, policy, theory and so on) and what has shaped and informed the production of knowledge.

We begin with what can often feel like the most challenging of stakeholders – the inspector. As outlined in Chapter 2, inspection systems can often feel difficult to understand and there are questions as to the difference that they can make in improving the quality of provision. Our first example, from Jacky, encourages us to take a different perspective – rather than feeling burdened by or questioning the relevance of the inspection system, take ownership of it.

Jacky: Quality is a Concept that Belongs to You

Quality is a 'concept'; its definition is personally constructed and therefore open to different interpretation. I interpret quality as the foundation upon which my practice is built; it must be robust when open to scrutiny, durable in consistency of approach and sufficiently resilient to meet the unexpected challenges of working with young children and their families.

Fundamental to developing a vision of quality for your practice is ensuring your vision is underpinned by the expectations set out in the

(Continued)

(Continued)

national Ofsted inspection framework. Reflecting on what is required to be an 'Outstanding' provider within this framework, I have concluded that it means the provider accepting responsibility for evidencing the quality of provision they offer, that is, not relying on others such as an inspector to seek it out. I recognise that this obligation doesn't sit comfortably with early years practitioners who, in my experience, tend to be quite reserved when talking about their good works. I squirm when asked to rate my practice on the Ofsted Self Evaluation Framework (SEF); there is a sense of boasting if you tick the 'Outstanding' box: 'my practice is exemplary'. It may be tempting to tick the 'Good' criteria: 'my practice is strong', however if you truly believe you are offering the highest quality provision you must be confident to publicly acknowledge this; the key is to do so with humility, not arrogance.

Confidence in the quality of your practice stems from understanding what is required of you; this means being aware of what the inspector is looking for and how this relates to the children in your care. Familiarity with these requirements means you are better prepared for an unannounced inspection visit. Not only will you be able to guide the inspector to the relevant evidence, but you will also speak the same 'quality' language with shared meaning. Further, having a common understanding of quality with the inspector enables you to showcase how your interpretation of quality builds on the generic expectation – the 'added value' that you offer which exceeds that expected of you. This is where you can set out how you differ to other 'Outstanding' providers; by identifying those special qualities that appeal so much to parents that they choose your practice over other providers.

I believe that being clear about your point of difference is equally as important as understanding the national expectations set out in the Ofsted inspection framework; it is the order of evidence presentation that places the framework in pole position. The provider's interpretation of quality is an important part of the continuous improvement cycle; what an inspector learns from you raises their awareness of practice and this, in turn, can be shared with others, helping to improve outcomes for increasingly more children.

There is, without doubt, huge potential for Ofsted and the early years sector to work together in a more collaborative manner. This requires the sector to take 'ownership' of the inspection framework and to engage in the overall process as an equal partner. There is scope to develop the existing interpretation of the 'quality' concept; however, this must be a quiet revolution in which all participants speak the same language with common meaning and shared understanding. Unfortunately, such a position is a far cry from the current, almost adversarial, relationship that exists between the parties.

Jacky's opening statement reflects what we have been looking at previously in this book. Quality is not something fixed, an enlightenment goal to be reached. It is a concept and one that is fluid and changeable. However, Jacky is aware of the realities of being an early years practitioner and that this comes with a series of expectations. The first of these expectations is that of meeting Ofsted requirements. Whilst we have looked to deconstruct, critique and problematise Ofsted in the previous chapters, we recognise that meeting external registration requirements is none-the-less an important feature of working in the early years. Whilst here we have looked at Ofsted in the context of being an early years provider in England, other parts of the UK as well as many other countries have similar external surveillance systems.

In Chapter 2, we considered the notion of external surveillance systems acting as a panoptic gaze, designed to regulate and control the provision of early years services, whilst here we see Jacky standing strong in this gaze. She does not look to hide from it, far from it; in fact, Jacky looks to take ownership of the inspection system. In an ideal world, policy makers would recognise that those with the most expertise in delivering quality early years services are early years practitioners, but until such a time when the early years sector is asked for its views, Jacky presents us with the idea that the inspection process is actually an opportunity to share your expertise. Understanding what is required of the inspection process offers the opportunity for you to consider how you meet a particular requirement. As we have stressed in earlier chapters, there is no one way to be an early years practitioner – there is huge variation in how early years providers operate. What is key is understanding why you do what you do, but, as Jacky suggests, on its own this is not enough. In thinking about why you do what you do, there is a need to be mindful of how this relates to what is expected of you. Knowing what is expected of you reflects the sense that we are in a time of accountability. This accountability is part of a wider 'what works' policy-making regime that we have discussed in earlier chapters. Through the inspection process, you are asked to demonstrate that you 'work' – that you are effective as a practitioner. It is a part of the managerial discourse (Osgood, 2006), but Jacky suggests that we do not need to feel oppressed by these requirements.

Jacky emphasises the importance of understanding the language of the inspection regime (Ofsted). If we think back to Chapter 2 where we began to explore post-structuralist perspectives and the notion of deconstruction, we can see a link to the use of language. Language is connected with the politics of knowledge and the production of discourses (MacNaughton, 2005). We outlined in Chapter 2 how 'discourses represent a way of viewing, thinking and speaking about the social world' in order to create normalised behaviour. The speaking part refers to the use of language – there are particular ways of speaking about given subject areas, such as the early years. Inspection systems, such as Ofsted, seek to create normalised ways of talking about the early years – they try to impose their language on us. Yet post-structuralism asks us to reflect on the language that is being used, to deconstruct it and to highlight where there are cracks and contradictions. It is the cracks that enable an interpretation of quality criteria rather than a dictation.

It is not possible to escape the panoptic gaze, but there is space to take ownership of it by using knowledge and expertise to demonstrate how practice responds to requirements. Given this, as we explore the following examples, we touch on the history and theory of early years provision to help illustrate how both of these are your friends in explaining why you do what you do. So, whether you are reading the case study examples or thinking of your own, it is worthwhile considering what Jacky has said above – how do your principles relate back to what an inspector will be looking for? How can you justify your perspective to someone who has never seen your setting before? How will you develop an understanding of quality that is right for you and your setting? We will identify with features from the EYFS during the following discussions as this is the curriculum that each of the practitioners is following, but we will ground it in the long history of pedagogical theory that is present in the early years to help explain that, often, what we deem to be a feature of quality is grounded in theory.

The Interplay of Structural and Process Features of Quality

In Chapter 1, we considered how quality is often defined in terms of structural and process features. Structural features include ratios, group size, staff education and training, material and space (see Gambaro et al., 2013; Munton et al., 2002) and are often favoured as they can be correlated with child outcomes. Structural features have a tendency to be rather static as they reflect the quantitative, modernist and positivist approaches to quality that can be measured and 'ticked off' on a checklist. However, structural features of quality do not work in isolation. There is evidence of a relationship between structural and process variables of quality (see Gambaro et al., 2013). As outlined by Munton et al. (2002), structural and process features interplay – you cannot take one away by adding more of the other. The balance between different features of quality was noted following the publication of More Great Childcare (DfE, 2013). In the document, the Conservative–Liberal Democrat coalition (2010–2015) proposed that adult/child ratios could be increased and that quality would not deteriorate if staff had higher qualification levels. Based on some selective international comparisons and part reading of research evidence, the premise was that higher qualified staff would be able to care for more children (Payler and Georgeson, 2014). However, Eisenstadt et al. (2013) published a document to illustrate that juggling features of quality in this way is not that simple. Different features of quality are associated with different child outcomes, so adjusting one feature and then balancing that against another could at best leave quality at the same level, but is not likely to increase it (Payler and Georgeson, 2014). More Great Childcare has helped highlight how complex quality is – it is a complete package. One important structural feature of quality is that of resources and the environment. How early years practitioners and leaders construct the environment and present resources within it is obviously important in regard to how children will engage with them, but how the environment is constructed also reflects principles relating to how children learn. In the next example, Sue considers how her principles around children as competent and capable have influenced how she likes to construct the environment, but enacting your principles does not just happen…

Sue: Enabling children to have ownership of the structure

The first thing I would say is that although the buildings, grounds and resources available to a setting clearly do have a big impact on quality, they are only one aspect of a complex issue. For me, the attitude of practitioners towards children is also key. I think that for quality to exist it is important that practitioners view children as competent and capable individuals and accord them the same rights as they accord adults. An example of how this looks in practice is trusting children with a wide range of art materials. In my previous setting we had a well-resourced craft area with a variety of paints, pens, scissors and glue freely available to the children. The children were taught how to use and care for these resources and they were trusted to use them sensibly. In my new setting all these resources were hidden in a cupboard when I first arrived. When I enquired as to why this was, I was informed by everyone that this was because the children needed to be supervised when using them. I, in my ignorance, of course assumed I knew better and

(Continued)

(Continued)

fetched them all out and put them where they could be seen. When I next looked there was felt pen everywhere and the pens had been put out of reach again. The temptation was to leave them out of reach but it was my own fault – I should have realised that children who have never had free rein with pens before would need support to get used to this idea. Needless to say the pens are back out again. This little episode also made me realise that practitioners who have been used to having more control over the resources children have access to will also need some support to get used to this type of freer approach.

I think that this type of free approach to activities and resources is actually very important in terms of quality because we know that for young children to learn effectively they need to be able to pursue their own interests. In quality settings the adults relinquish control over learning and instead of leading learning they follow the child's lead. This approach requires a high degree of flexibility, especially in group settings where practitioners have to be able to respond to the different needs and interests of a number of children at the same time. In fact, I think working in a quality pre-school setting may be a bit like taking part in a very complex dance where you have to partner everyone in the room but only the children can hear the music and each child's music has a different beat. Really good practitioners can move swiftly and lightly between many different partners over the course of the day, quickly adjusting to the different steps and rhythms of each child. Working in this way not only requires flexibility, it also requires practitioners to have a high tolerance for change and uncertainty because the dance is different each day and it changes and evolves as the children grow and develop. In my old setting the practitioners were very good at this dance and it was a given that nothing stayed the same for very long. We were constantly reflecting on how the children were responding to the routines, resources and activities and if we felt something was not working for the children we changed it. It did however take a long time to establish this way of working and it certainly helped that I had a relatively stable core of people who worked with me for many years and who shared my core beliefs about children.

Sue presents us with an example of how we can consider the interplay between structural and process features of quality. Structural features are the resources, whilst the process is considering how they are incorporated and utilised within the pedagogical practice of the setting. For Sue, as with all of the practitioners, giving the child autonomy is an important feature of early years practice, whether it is phrased as following their interests, enabling them to take the lead in their play, meeting their needs, being child centred or a combination of these things. The autonomous child is a child with social agency (see Chapter 2), no matter how you refer to it – the principle is that children have a voice and are active in constructing their lives (Jenks, 2004). Biological immaturity might be a fact, but how we understand and construct this does not mean we treat children as being immature (James and Prout, 1997). The construction of the autonomous child has grown in prominence in the last 30 to 40 years with the rise of the sociology of childhood. Equally, developments in children's rights have been instrumental in shaping understandings of children and childhood in regard to their autonomy and voice.

A key aspect of the sociology of childhood is the recognition that childhood is socially constructed and therefore shaped by the culture and time in which people are located. It relates back to what we have said about discourses and the use of language – particular ways of viewing and speaking about the early years have been constructed through time and with the influence of various stakeholders. However, as time shifts this does not mean that old perceptions of childhood disappear, rather they are reconstructed in a way that makes them feel relevant for now. The reason that we raise this is that a number of early years pioneers were writing during the industrial revolution. At this time, there was a rejection of children working in paid employment, particularly where it was regarded as dangerous, by philanthropists who were driven by a romantic notion of childhood whereby children needed nurturing and protecting from the harsh realities of the industrial world (Hendrick, 1997). Part of rejecting an association between the industrial world and childhood gave fuel to a concept of children being close to nature. Writers such as Rousseau, Froebel and Isaacs all upheld principles of the importance of nature in supporting children's development (Selbie et al., 2015). They all also believed in the child being the leader of their learning – the autonomous child. It is an example of the production of knowledge and the creation of language to talk about children, childhood and early years and how they evolve over time. The starting point for a child who leads their learning can be linked to a rejection of the industrial revolution, but over time and through further research links have been made between autonomy and approaches to learning.

For us, the rise in the sociology of childhood and understandings of children's rights, along with developments in how childhood has been seen throughout history and a growth in understanding of how children learn, have been important features in shaping early years practice. The legacy of these early years pioneers is still evident today, not only in regard to a philosophy of early years pedagogical practice, but also in relation to how these philosophies have shaped and informed curriculum documents such as the EYFS. Within the EYFS (DfE, 2014), there is reference to enabling environments, differentiated learning and the unique child as three of the four guiding principles (we will look at the fourth – positive relationships – later). The characteristic of effective teaching and learning also lists active learning. All of these relate to Sue leaving out drawing materials for the children to freely engage with. What we have looked to consider is what has shaped and informed a belief that pens should be left out so that children can have autonomy in their playing and learning. The construction of knowledge around the autonomous child has many different influences and we have only touched on some of what we feel are the key ones. However, it is an example of what we discussed earlier in this chapter about understanding what and who is informing your practice and how this shapes the ways in which we speak about early years practice. It is not about deconstructing the knowledge that exists so that there is nothing left, rather sometimes it is about deconstructing so that you better understand your beliefs and can share them with others, whether that is the Ofsted inspector, as raised by Jacky, or the team that you work with, as touched on by Sue and as we explore further later.

In linking back to Jacky's discussion of the Ofsted inspection, we can also see how at times there are tensions between those discourses that look to govern how quality early years practice is understood and what shapes and informs practice. Whilst the EYFS refers to the autonomous child who leads their learning, this feels at odds with developments in England that have led to a preoccupation with assessing children. Two year old checks, Foundation Stage profiles and baseline assessments are all hotly debated as the assessment of children within them contradicts the ideology of supporting the unique child, the former representing a 'what works' discourse and the latter the autonomous child. Roberts-Holmes (2014) has written about how bureaucracy and top-down pressures such as those represented by Ofsted can lead practitioners to feel that their practice is being constrained – they are not able to uphold the autonomous child. However, as early years practitioners, we have to make sense of early years policy and, as Campbell-Barr (2015) highlights, there is a process of interpretation when a practitioner puts policy into practice. Through drawing on knowledge of the role of play and the outdoors, for example, we can explain why we do what we do. The early years pioneers have passed on their thinking (Pound, 2011) and we can use this in support of pedagogical practice. Therefore, for Sue, there is much to support her beliefs and to enable her to explain her approach to her new colleagues, but developing a team approach of common principles can take time.

Staffing

As we have explored in all of the preceding chapters, staffing (whether a leader or not) is central to the quality of provision. Yet staffing is a broad category as it can encompass the number of staff, qualification levels, experience and teamwork. Within each of these areas, there are a number of complexities – for example, when we talk of qualifications, what is it about a given qualification that enables us to support the delivery of a quality early years environment? Equally, there is an interrelationship between these features – for example, how people with different experiences come together to work as a team. In Sue's discussion, she raised the idea of a complex dance, one where children and adults can be moving to a different beat and yet skilled practitioners can still find a way of gliding around the dance floor. Selbie et al. (2015) comment on how a skilled practitioner can often look effortless in their practice and Georgeson et al. (2014) coined the phased 'watchfulness' to exemplify the practitioner who seems to be watching children play from a distance, often appearing uninvolved, but who is actually carefully observing to inform when to intervene to extend a child's learning or to foster relationships between children (even when this relates to squabbles around turn taking). In Sandra's discussion of quality, we see that qualifications and professional development, experience and teamwork are all important for her understanding of quality and that it is the combination of these things that makes for a skilled and effective workforce.

Sandra: Qualifications and Experience

I have had Early Years Professional Status since 2009 and I feel that gaining this qualification has given me the confidence not only to lead the team but also to stand up for the things that are important to the setting. It is easy to get sucked into what others see as quality and then have a confused or blurred vision of the way forward. This can happen when stakeholders expect you to share their vision of what quality looks like and as a leader you have to maintain a balance between what is conforming practice and transforming practice. It would be easy to do things without question just because it is a requirement or suggestion from a stakeholder. There are statutory requirements that have to be adhered to and then there is practice guidance and also what is considered best practice. The children and families in our area have their own peculiar family cultures and without knowledge of these cultures how can decisions be made on what is best practice for our children?

(Continued)

(Continued)

I feel that the team have confidence in my knowledge and also that I am a role model for their own professional development. Encouraging staff members to follow their own particular interests in child development through training and experience is important to developing a good quality childcare team. We will discuss aspects of my professional development and their own and reflect on how we can use our new ideas and knowledge within the setting. It is a shared experience.

Experience is a very valuable asset to any setting and I am fortunate to have a very experienced Assistant Manager who is also the setting's Child Protection Officer; she has a wealth of experience with supporting families who have had children at the setting. I rely on her knowledge of child protection and family issues and what often seems like a sixth sense or gut instinct regarding problem families. Courage is often required when dealing with suspected child protection issues, particularly when confronting parents, and a strength of commitment to keep the child at the centre of everything we do. I know that we have the same vision for the setting and we have both grown with the setting, have lived its history and planned its future. Qualifications are an indicator of quality within early years leadership but experience also counts and I believe that qualifications alone are not enough to indicate quality in a leader.

In Sandra's account of quality, we can see parallels with Jacky's in that there is recognition of the external pressures of stakeholders when developing an understanding of quality. Sandra refers to this as the 'conforming practice', but acknowledges the importance of not being 'sucked in' by the expectations of external stakeholders such as Ofsted. Sandra's response to inspection is perhaps a little more subversive than Jacky's, but the principle is the same – believe in what you do.

For Sandra, the needs of the families that she works with are important. As we outlined in the introduction to Part Three, the area in which Sandra is based is one that is classified as being economically deprived and this can bring with it many challenges. A project exploring the features of good quality provision for 2-year-olds (Georgeson et al., 2014) highlighted the notion that supporting and working with families can be challenging. In particular, Georgeson et al. explored issues around providing quality early years provision as part of the free early education entitlement for disadvantaged 2-year-olds. The project highlighted that working with those who are experiencing some form of disadvantage can create additional pressures, such as additional time being needed to support these families and staff possessing emotional resilience when working with families with complex lives. What Sandra's writing highlights (and that of Georgeson et al., 2014) is the importance of developing practice that supports the families in the community you work in. This means that what might work for an early years setting in Kensington, London, is likely to be different to what works in a setting in Looe, Cornwall. In responding to the needs of stakeholders, it can feel like a juggling act whereby parents, Ofsted, the local authority and any number of other stakeholders are all making demands of us, as outlined in our discussion in Chapter 4 regarding the many accountabilities of an early years leader. But again, working with families is a feature of the EYFS and so knowing and understanding your families is important.

Qualifications

Sandra also emphasises the knowledge that she has gained from her qualifications. It is well established that qualifications are associated with the quality of provision. Findings from the EPPE project helped to inform the development of Early Years Professional Status (now the Early Years Teacher, see Payler and Georgeson, 2014) in light of the association found in the data between qualifications and quality. Whilst policy has not always upheld its commitment to a graduate workforce, as we outlined in the previous chapter, and there have been calls to ensure that qualifications are robust and fit for purpose (Nutbrown, 2012), it is established that qualifications matter (Jones, 2014). However, the evidence around qualifications presents us with a challenge – what is it about a qualification that leads to quality? As Jones (2014) has suggested, it is not just the qualification, but also knowing what to do that leads to quality. The idea of knowing what to do inevitably implies that experience can help. Georgeson et al. (2014), referred to earlier, demonstrate that there is a complex set of skills that early years practitioners believe are needed to support quality provision – these relate to qualifications and experience, but also to dispositions – a set of innate skills that someone possesses – and if we think back to Chapter 2, we can also see that other research has highlighted the importance of dispositions in the workforce. We can see the idea of dispositions in what Sandra has said above. In some ways, dispositions run the risk of undermining professionalisation agendas and potentially reinforce gender stereotypes (the idea that women are natural carers and caring comes from within), as mentioned in the last chapter. However, there is much to challenge the concept of early years being suited to women (Cameron, 2006). Rather, as with many other forms of employment, people will have their strengths in different areas. As Sandra has highlighted, it is about identifying those strengths and using them to the advantage of the setting. Equally, it is about sharing knowledge, whether it is about an individual family or something learnt on a course, amongst the team.

What we feel Sandra's discussion highlights is the importance of thinking about different forms of knowledge and how they shape and inform early years practice. Sandra refers to the 'peculiar family cultures' in the area that she works and the knowledge that she and her team have regarding this, but equally she discusses the knowledge gained from qualifications and that which comes from dispositions. Often, knowledge is perceived as that which is written down, whether in a child development book or a policy document, but there are different forms of knowledge. Eraut (2000) explores how there are different forms of knowledge that are acquired in different ways. There is the knowledge that is derived from the academic literature and from policy that can be seen as codified, scientific knowledge, but there is also cultural knowledge (Georgeson et al., 2014), some of which may be written down, but often not. Cultural knowledge can relate to whether using a dummy is seen as appropriate, or to whether a child is seen as having a tantrum or testing their boundaries. As Sandra notes, in the early years, there is an interaction between the knowledge of the parents, what you know about the parents and codified knowledge. Again, we can see how considering where knowledge has come from can help in understanding it, but we also have to be mindful that all forms of knowledge have a contribution to make, just in different ways and in different forms for different people.

Your Principles Based on the Needs of the Child

One of the features that is apparent in all of the case study examples is that the practitioners have strong principles and this is also true of the last example from Cheryl. However, Cheryl also reminds us that this is difficult when we are looking to create principles for a term – quality – that is so slippery to define, let alone understand.

> ### Cheryl: Creating an Ethos
>
> I feel that quality is a term often used in early years and although we recognise quality when we see it, it is difficult to describe. I looked it up in the Oxford English Dictionary to try and find a definition and found that quality was described in five different contexts: as a degree of excellence; a faculty, skill or accomplishment; a high rank; being affirmative
>
> *(Continued)*

(Continued)

(or negative); and distinctive character. I think that in many ways quality in the early years could be viewed as a combination of these attributes. A degree of excellence indicates a measurable, comparable standard, and this is reflected in the benchmarks of Ofsted inspection outcomes. However, quality is not always a tangible commodity – it is about a setting's ethos, the reflective practice of the staff team and strong leadership. It is the attributes which motivate and guide us and form the principles that we believe in that I would like to discuss.

Quality provision relates to skills, confidence and commitment to the child. Having a good understanding of child development, recognising that all experiences are learning opportunities and, most important in my view, being able to look at the world through the eyes of the child means we can recognise the value of providing holistic learning environments for all children. We often talk about best practice when considering quality in the early years, however that also seems to suggest one size fits all, whereas I would argue that the pedagogical skill is in being able to make the best decisions at any given time, and it would be better to describe this as wise practice.

The ethos or distinctive character of the setting has to be shared with staff and other adults, include the children and be embedded in working practice. However, building this shared vision has to be based on sound knowledge of children's learning and development. It takes agreement, time, reflection and continued professional development. An open professional approach within the staff team can lead to shared understanding and consistent improvement of practice and provision. For example, when discussing the environment and resources that we provide, open-ended resources were considered important. However, we still needed to agree what we, as a team, understand by open-ended resources, why they are beneficial, and reflect on Nicholson's theory of loose parts and how this is embedded in our pedagogical values when working with the children. This collaborative process incorporates staff ideas, is underpinned by theory and provides a basis for the rationale that shapes our ethos.

Cheryl's overview of quality brings together what we have seen in the other three examples – the autonomous child, teamwork, quality being much more than a set of predetermined indicators and an ethos. Whilst we have considered the first two in this chapter and the third is a theme that we see throughout the book, the notion of an ethos is not something that we have fully addressed, but it is pivotal to how we lead quality early years provision.

As we have explored in earlier chapters, we all hold strong views about children: who they are and what they can do – and childhood: what makes a good childhood. Understanding what you think is good for children will inform who you are as an early years practitioner. As Wickett and Selbie (2015) outline, beliefs as to who children are, how they learn and the role of the child in the learning process will guide interactions with children. The example from Sue demonstrated a commonly held view of the autonomous child and we explored how this related to historical and theoretical thinking around children and childhood. Wickett and Selbie (2015) also look at how pioneers in the early years have shaped and informed thinking about early years practice and the way in which early years practice is understood. The process of understanding why you do what you do is what will help to explain your approach to those who wish to question your practice, whether that is a parent visiting the setting for the first time or an inspector, whilst equally it can help develop your own understanding. This is where reflecting on your understanding and knowledge is important.

> **Reflection Point**
>
> Take the time to write down what you think constitutes quality in the provision of early years services. Consider what has informed your understanding – are there any aspects that you would like to explore further to see where your understanding may have come from?

Chapter Summary

In this chapter, we have considered the views and experiences of quality of four early years leaders. We have explored what has shaped and informed the views of these leaders in order to highlight the construction of knowledge and language to inform early years practice. Recognising who and what is shaping our practice is important as it can help us to understand our values and beliefs. We can see in all of the early years practitioners the importance of principles in guiding what they do and we have considered the role of history, sociology, early years pioneers and policy in shaping the principles behind early years practice. Whilst in previous chapters we have been critical of policy, we have seen that in some instances the ideas of policy can relate to the principles of early years leaders. In looking to the

(Continued)

(Continued)

next chapter where we consider reflective practice, reflecting on early years principles and understandings of quality and leadership is not about deconstructing things until there is nothing left, but about being aware of what is shaping early years practice.

Further Reading

Brooker, L. (2011) 'Developing dispositions for life', in T. Waller, J. Whitmarsh and K. Clarke (eds), *The Power of Ideas: Making Sense of Theory and Practice in Early Childhood*. Maidenhead: Open University Press, pp. 83–98.

This chapter explores how our understandings of dispositions have evolved over time and how they can shape and inform our practice.

Pound, L. (2014) 'Playing, learning and developing', in J. Moyles, J. Payler and J. Georgeson (eds), *Early Years Foundations: Critical Issues*. Maidenhead: Open University Press, pp. 19–29.

This chapter is helpful in reminding readers of the connection between early years pioneers and current early years practice. The chapter acknowledges the challenges that those in practice can find with curriculum documents. In particular we like the focus on 'joyful, playful and enabling' learning.

REFLECTING ON LEADING QUALITY EARLY YEARS SERVICES

> **Chapter Overview**
>
> This chapter seeks to build on Chapter 5 by identifying challenges that our four case study practitioners have encountered in their working lives. We asked them to reflect on a challenge within their setting and discuss how they use reflective processes within their practice and encourage the same with their staff team. In this chapter, we will explore the individual accounts and the powerful insights that the reflections offered the practitioner. We will also look at the different ways in which the practitioners have used reflective processes, what emerges from all four accounts as key issues for practice and how their reflective capacity has enhanced their understanding and practice of their settings. It is our intention that the exploration and examination of different approaches will be useful for you to reflect on your own understandings of quality and leadership and then to build on these in relation to your co-workers and the families that access your setting.

First, we should acknowledge our own strong belief that engaging in reflection is a powerful and important activity that enables deeper understanding which in turn allows for well-informed, secure practice and considerable personal and professional development. We would argue that engaging in reflective practice enables any practitioner to move from being a competent technician to being a creative, thoughtful and proactive professional who is able to think deeply about their work and make meaningful interventions in the lives of the children and families they work with. Crawford (2014: 8) talks about the development of a 'personal leadership framework' through the use of reflective activity as a process focusing on thoughts, knowledge, emotions and experience to inform current practice and construct new ideas and innovative strategies for the future. Using reflection to construct your own understanding of quality and leadership in relation to the families that you work with is central to what we have been saying throughout this book in relation to post-structuralist perspectives. In developing your understanding of quality and leadership, it is important to reflect on what and who has shaped that understanding. Reflection can allow you to make sense of why you believe certain aspects of your practice are important or why you might feel particularly frustrated by policy makers, for example. We are not alone in our belief in the importance of reflection; for many years practitioners have been encouraged to engage in reflexivity (thinking about events that have occurred and debating the actions, motivations, thoughts and feelings that they evoke and asking questions as to their significance) as a way of ensuring mindful behaviour and thinking that enables sustainable decision making and development of services. There has been a great deal written about the power and desirability of reflexivity. For example, Bourdieu (1992) regarded reflexivity as an important opportunity to challenge our preconceptions, prejudices and unthinking actions, which will result in a thoughtful and clear sense of purpose which is free from any hidden bias that might impact negatively on our actions. More recently, Attard (2008) argues that reflective practice allows us to find and embrace the creativity that exists within any uncertainty we find ourselves immersed in; to be alive to the myriad of possibilities that are available whilst remaining sensitive to those around us.

Post-structuralist perspectives complement and extend the role of reflection in contemplating our thoughts and feelings, challenging preconceptions and considering opportunities, towards a model that looks to understand what has shaped those thoughts, feelings and preconceptions. Post-structuralism enables an analysis of the power dynamics that influence quality and leadership in the early years and challenges the notion of 'truths' – one way of thinking about and implementing quality and leadership – in favour of a model that accepts there is no one (correct) approach (MacNaughton, 2005). Critical reflection can make apparent previously hidden ideologies that seek to shape the way early years practitioners think and work. As we have discussed in the previous chapter, the deconstructive nature of post-structuralism can feel as if we break everything down until there is nothing left. The same can be said for reflection – the challenging of preconceptions and beliefs runs the risk of shaking the very foundations of what is regarded as good early years pedagogy and our role in performing and shaping it. However, we are keen to stress that reflection, whether via a post-structuralist lens or one that looks to adopt another model, is not always about challenge in a negative sense. Rather, reflection provides opportunities to better understand early years quality and leadership as a mechanism for feeling more confident and powerful in the working role. We also believe, as MacNaughton (2005: 228) has outlined, that reflection 'requires educators to take control of their own learning and meaning making'. What we go on to present is a range of ways of approaching reflection. Whilst we encourage you, the reader, to think about power dynamics within your reflections, this may be something that you want to works towards over time.

If we need further encouragement to engage in reflective practice, we know that there is a substantial, embedded heritage of reflective practice in health and social work that has recently been embraced by the lexicon of early years practice. It is fair to say that reflective practice has formed the habitus of early years practice; it has become the custom, disposition and structure of the workplace which has been supported by a number of policies signalling the value of reflective practice in the modern early years sector. Reflective practice can be seen as part of the discourse of early years pedagogy as early years practitioners are moulded into thinking and believing that reflection is *just what happens* in the early years. As we explored in the previous chapter, there are some features of the discursive production of early years that we feel are helpful, but there is still a need to be mindful of who and what is shaping these ways of thinking in order to appreciate whether there is shared understanding. One of the most persuasive change agents in the development of reflective practice was the National Professional Qualification in Integrated Centre Leadership (NPQICL; NCSL, 2004) which sought to equip leaders in the sector with key leadership skills and knowledge through teaching and learning mechanisms that promoted the ideology of 'leadership within' and the desirability of reflective practice in the workplace. Further actions to embed reflective practice have been the development of standards for leaders of settings, for the Early Years Professional (EYP) and, most recently, the Early Years Educator and Early Years Teacher (NCTL, 2013) via the teaching standards (Teaching Agency, 2013). Research has endorsed the desirability of reflective practice. The recent Effective Pre-School, Primary and Secondary Education (EPPSE) Report (Sylva et al., 2014) makes clear how important quality settings are to the well-being and future achievement of children, and Hayes et al. (2014) argue that only through having staff that are critically reflective might this be achieved. However, we are not convinced that the definition of reflection that is used by external agencies charged with making comments on the quality of the setting or on the suitability of the leadership and team processes, embraces fully the concept of deep, informed reflexivity that the literature recommends as enabling the move from technical competence to creative professionalism (Sheppard, 1995).

Models of Reflection

There are numerous ways in which practitioners might reflect on their practice with many models of reflection being firmly embedded in the reflective landscape – such as Kolb's (1984) cyclical model of experience, reflect, conceptualise, experiment, experience and Gibbs' (1988) model, also cyclical, of description, feeling, evaluation, analysis, conclusion and action plan. Novice reflectors find the existence of such models useful as they start learning how to reflect. Their model of choice will allow them to work systematically through the different aspects of their experience, bringing into consciousness their thoughts, feelings, assumptions and prejudices that might then be further reflected on in terms of challenge, context, meaning and significance. What is important is that novice reflectors are encouraged to use the model that makes the most sense to them in order to develop their own reflective style, working with confidence towards developing a deeply enquiring reflective mode which enables them to move from a simple diary entry to a closer, more detailed scrutiny of the activities, perspectives, consequences and actions encompassed by their daily activities. This close scrutiny enables informed decisions to be made as to what changes might be needed or could be useful; what has been good practice and should be preserved at all costs; and why it might be that conversations, actions and decisions have taken shape in a particular way. Thus, reflection is more than simply thinking about what has happened and what was right or wrong, what went well and what did not. Engaging in reflective activity enables a close look at the motivations, thoughts and feelings that have informed every action, and explores what has shaped that understanding and who or what has tried to influence that way of thinking or acting. In reflecting on our understanding, it is possible to think about how it might be used in the future. What reflection should *not* be is a mechanism for criticising and thereby disabling the actions, thoughts and feelings of the reflector. All too often, reflective activity can start a cycle of self-criticism that is unhelpful; asking oneself what did not go well and why that might be makes practitioners anxious and they can begin to lose their confidence. We see this clearly articulated in Jacky's work and discuss it further later in this chapter.

Neither should reflection be 'cosy', seeking to validate, applaud or praise the actions of the reflector without scrutiny, awarding merit points without justification and creating a false picture of ability or skill that can be dangerous to the individual and the people they work with. Reflection can take place in many different ways – from the more usual activity of writing things down, either free flow or using one of the many models of reflection available, to the use of visual or aural images, meditation or physical movement. Reflective activity does not have to involve the written word; reflectors can use whatever mechanisms make most sense to them – visual methods such as drawings, diagrams, models, sculptures, films, using clay, pens or video packages; aural methods, using music or sound; or tactile such as using fabrics or multi-textured materials. One of the main purposes of engaging in reflective activity is to make visible one's inner thoughts and feelings about a situation or circumstance that may not be noticed otherwise, as our busy lives prevent us from being aware of what we have observed, worried about, been pleased about or thought fleetingly we must do something about. Reflective practice is (most often) a deeply personal activity where one works on the observations and records that have been made in terms of making visible the underlying issues that are not immediately apparent. Any subsequent action plan is thus well thought through, highly developed and an authentic response to the situation. It can also be a joint venture where people reflect in pairs, groups or teams, developing an in-depth dialogue and, ultimately, a shared understanding of the issue at hand. As a team-building exercise, shared reflections can be a useful tool for mutual understanding and joint action planning. Yet reflection can also go beyond the individual person, pair or team to consider the influence of society and policy in shaping thoughts and feelings. In reflecting on daily observations, it is important to recognise that they take place within a social context where preconceived societal norms as to what is 'right' and 'normal' seek to inform early years practice. This might be the developmental discourse that informs understanding of a child's ability or gender discourses that shape views on what is an appropriate action for boys and girls. Within the early years, we feel that there is often a predisposition to push against the potentially controlling nature of social norms, such as with the recognition that children develop at different rates and in their own ways; and that girls and boys can choose equally to access all resources in the setting – whether cars or dolls. However, we recognise that not all people will think in the same ways (nor do we think that they should), so often taking the reflection beyond the individual, to incorporate the team, is about drawing on the social to appreciate why there are different values and beliefs about early years practice, helping to come to some form of shared vision. We see the role of the team, as well as individual reflections, in the case study examples below.

Reflective Accounts of Leadership Challenge

We asked our four leaders to think about challenges they had recently faced in their leadership and to record and reflect, in any way that felt comfortable, their thoughts, feelings, actions and any identified subsequent dynamics. The purpose of the exercise was to further develop thinking about the leadership of quality started in Chapter 5 with a deeper exploration of some of the challenges that ensue. Navigating successfully through a critical challenge can be seen as a hallmark of good leadership practice, and the capacity of a leader to reflect on their actions is an important indicator of the quality of a setting.

The Importance of Emotional Well-being for Leaders

Jacky uses her reflection to explore an often ignored aspect of leadership – the importance of the emotional well-being of the leader. As discussed in Chapter 4, the amount of emotional labour involved in working in an early years setting can demand a great deal from a practitioner, sometimes more than they can give. The emotional work required of staff members has been well documented and discussed. The emotional impact of the work on leaders, has been less discussed, so Jacky's account is highly relevant for us to explore. Jacky tells us how vital it is to be aware of any feelings of unease, disquiet and anxiety and to make appropriate and effective action plans to address the issues they highlight or raise. Her account also advises against reactive, non-reflective decision making, advocating instead for reflective thinking that enables a process of proactive activity. She also highlights the use of literature and theory to inform that process. Jacky finds some of her answer in a book written by a teacher about how the dynamics within a classroom will shift over time and she is able to make a connection between the book and Tuckman's (1965) stages of group development. Research on reflective practice has shown that many professionals do not see the relationship between theory and practice (Ruch, 2002; Saltiel, 2003), meaning that knowledge becomes divorced from experience – what Schön (1983) calls technical rationality where values, prejudices and assumptions go unnoticed and unchallenged. Poor practice, even dangerous practice, may well ensue as no one has taken the time to reflect, think and plan, and thus their decision-making process may be flawed and ineffective. Had Jacky not used the theoretical frameworks she chose to employ, her action plan may have been quite different and may have been less appropriate and helpful to the children and staff. The utilisation of theory enables her to know that what she has in place is effective and that she can trust that knowledge to support her planning for the gradual integration of the new children into the setting, as well as reinforcing her awareness that trying to rush or circumvent a very essential, developmental process could be harmful and/or could do the reverse of what she wishes to achieve – a happy cohesive learning community. Thus, through her writing, Jacky is able to pinpoint in more detail the exact source of her unease – a group of children who are unsettled, new to the setting and needing time to establish their relationships with each other, with the staff group and with the setting itself. She establishes, through her reflective process and by using her prior experience and her knowledge of theory, that this is normal behaviour and whilst she should not be complacent (the course of any stage of group development should be supported to prevent problems and enable shift to the next stage), she is able to acknowledge that it will change, there will be a shift in the group dynamics towards a state of equilibrium and harmony, similar but not exactly the same, as that which existed before.

What is fascinating is Jacky's awareness through the reflective process that part of her feeling of unease with this new group is that she is missing her previous group of children who have now left and gone to school. She writes of the 'rich and fertile learning environment' that she enjoyed with the previous group, hinting at an anxiety that she may not achieve the same with the new children. It is the nature of the sector that there is a continually shifting landscape of new children entering the group and shifting the dynamics. Furthermore, this shift tends to happen in large chunks with children leaving at the end of one academic year and others starting at the beginning of the next, and only a few joining at odd times of the year depending on birthdays, families moving home and so on. Leaders are therefore constantly engaged in supporting their staff in planning for new intakes, developing new relationships with children and creating the optimum learning environment for each new cohort of different personalities, learning styles and needs. There is also a need to acknowledge the grief process that is also going on with staff feeling sad at the loss of children in whom they have invested time and emotion. There will have been a deep sense of attachment to that group of children which, in line with bereavement theory (Freud, 1917; Kübler-Ross, 1969; Stroebe and Schut, 1999), will have to be worked through in order that the new group of children can experience the same level of emotional investment and commitment as the previous group. We talked in Chapter 4 about the emotional labour involved in early years work and Jacky's account demonstrates the impact of caring about and for the children and the workforce.

Furthermore, the process of ebb and flow, the continual checking of the dynamics of the learning environment, is challenging and demanding, both emotionally and practically. We would suggest that this has powerful implications for constructs of quality and leadership; as we have suggested throughout the book, they have to be dynamic and contextual, fluid and adaptable. A reflective leader is able to use experience from the past to inform the present and predict the future, in order to be confident and to plan effectively for their settings. Fluid and adaptable concepts of quality and leadership enable this process to happen, working within the ebb and flow of relationships, situations and events that characterise work in the early years sector. Fixed and firmly adhered to notions of quality and leadership will not be responsive to the changing needs of the setting and will ultimately lead to poor quality and to questions about the suitability and success of the leadership. Views about good practice might come from the same core – we may be able to apply the principle of adapting what we think is good for children to be relevant for the children we work with to thinking about leading quality. However, how we adapt thinking about leadership and quality needs to be relevant to the setting, the staff and the children we are working with. This idea is also clearly articulated through Sue's work later in this chapter, where she adapts her deeply principled thinking about the value of the outside environment to the needs and requirements, limitations and constraints of a new setting with different staff and children. Equally, in the previous chapter we could see that principles were key in guiding the case study practitioners in developing the quality of their settings. For example, as in Chapter 5, Jacky shows her capacity to question the expectation of externally imposed concepts of quality, creating and developing her own that are fit for purpose and effective in creating that rich learning environment that she places a high premium on establishing. In looking at Jacky's reflection, we can see the influence of child development discourse on informing her thinking and creating a common core to her practice, but, as outlined in the previous chapter, not all constructions of early years pedagogy have to be viewed as restrictive. Here the child development discourse is facilitating Jacky to make sense of the ebb and flow of an early years setting. The discourse is not prescriptive, rather it helps makes sense of the rhythms of an early years setting and informs her response to the challenge she has identified.

> ## Jackie – Challenge
>
> A hidden and often unspoken challenge to the provision of high quality early education and childcare provision is to be found, I believe, in the 'emotional well-being' of the leader: without this it is impossible to critically reflect on practice, the key to driving up quality.
>
> A few years ago I found myself in a situation where the group of children attending my practice were unsettled and I couldn't identify the reason for this. It was a subtle concern; a less experienced practitioner might not have picked up on it, however I had a feeling that the sessions could have gone better, my reflection on action skills kicking in, skills honed over the years. I found the answer, quite unexpectedly, in a book I was reading about a year in the life of an experienced teacher. The book described the teacher's feelings about her class at different points in time and how the dynamics of the group changed over the course of the year. Reflecting on this, I made a connection between my nagging doubts and the Stages of Group Development, identified as forming, storming, norming, performing and mourning, a construct that I had encountered on a previous project management training course.
>
> My feelings of unease were from the dynamics of a new group of children coming together, finding out about each other and testing the boundaries of the practice. My awareness of this challenging stage was heightened because it followed the calmer 'forming' stage at the beginning of term during which the children were finding their way in a new environment and becoming familiar with the rhythm and routines of their sessions. Looking back, I also identified that my thoughts were influenced by my experiences of the previous group of children, those who had left my practice for formal schooling. During the summer term the group had progressed to the 'performing' stage; they were a happy group that worked well together, creating a rich and fertile learning environment. My current children were not yet at this stage of group development.
>
> In due course all groups will move into the 'norming' stage where teamwork, respect for each other and collaborative experiences begin to emerge. This then develops into the 'performing' stage, that wonderful period where the children 'own' their learning and development,
>
> *(Continued)*

(Continued)

shaping and directing their play through creative thought and independent selection of resources. Each of the stages of group development is important to the children's learning and development. The challenge for the practitioner is to refrain from wishing that the valuable 'storming' stage will pass quickly. In 'child time', which always seems to pass more quickly than standard time, the 'norming' and 'performing' stages fly by and all too quickly 'mourning' arrives. This is the transition period into formal schooling which should be marked as a celebration of the children's progress.

Understanding potential flashpoints in practice and potential periods of high challenge helps you to develop coping strategies. This is a good time for team-bonding activities and to ensure on a personal level that you take time out to recharge your emotional well-being, thus maintaining and building on the quality of your practice.

Working in Partnership with Parents

In her account, Sandra looks at the challenge of involving parents in the setting and reflects on the activities of her team in encouraging and promoting a sense of shared ownership. We have already discussed in Chapter 4 the pressure of the expectation that leaders will not only interact with parents as partners in caring for their child, but actively encourage those who are 'hard to reach' to become similarly engaged. Sandra is accepting of the parents who do not want to be involved, she does not demonise them as uncaring or disinterested which is very easy to do, especially when involving parents has been set as an important objective and indicator of quality for all settings (DCSF, 2008; DfE, 2014). Sandra demonstrates through her reflection an empathic understanding of why it might be difficult for some parents to engage with the setting and to feel confident in taking a perspective of shared ownership in the learning activities their child is involved in. Through her reflective stance, Sandra is not only able to think about what is expected of her in policy terms and what she will be held accountable for in inspections and quality audits, but also to take ownership of the processes of her setting by understanding why she does what she does and recognising that she (and her staff) can only do their best. She can demonstrate good leadership through encouraging her staff to present parents with a myriad of opportunities for engagement, but she is able to acknowledge that it may not always be successful and that there are good reasons why that might be the case, and thus that it is OK for some families to decline engagement with the setting. This acceptance of a parent's perspective is important as the directive to work in partnership would appear to deny any right of self-determination, leading to a lot of time and energy being wasted by leaders and settings on trying to force the issue or feel guilty for 'failing' to get families involved. Douglass and Gittell (2012: 268) talk about the 'relational bureaucracy of professional practice' that is a top-down directive at odds with a setting's commitment to the development of caring, nurturing relationships with families. This relational bureaucracy is also seen in Greenfield's work (2012) where she explores the impact of perceived power differentials between staff and parents on the subsequent relationship they are able to develop. Through Sandra's reflective work, she is able to identify and understand why parents might not wish to be involved which could help her to create an action plan to attempt to ameliorate that situation or to move on and do other activities that will benefit the whole group (which may, by the release of pressure, enable the reluctant or anxious parent to join in). By bringing this issue into consciousness, her thinking about parental involvement will enable her to argue her position when asked to account for the levels of parental involvement in her setting, and to take ownership of the ways she and her staff work with the families in their care and of the quality of their relationships. This is extremely powerful and enables Sandra to feel strong in the panoptic gaze of external surveillance and to lead authentically and appropriately for her community.

Towards the end of her account, Sandra shows awareness that the measures she and her staff are putting in place are helping, that more parents are becoming involved and starting to feel more confident in their relationships within the setting. What is most illuminating is the importance of relationships: 'Perhaps because trust is there and they (parents) know that they can approach any one of the team at any time they don't feel the need to do any more.' She is hinting at the emotional work involved in engaging with families and beginning to show an awareness of the closeness they have engendered as a culture – where families feel cared for and know that they will be responded to when they need support or questions answered. Sandra is suggesting that you can have lots of systems for keeping in touch and many open days, coffee mornings and fetes, but the important foundation for partnership lies in the development of trusting, accessible relationships between staff and parents. Her disclosure of this detail in her reflective writing shifts her awareness to a different dimension – from the top-down relational bureaucracy identified earlier to a bottom-up, more nourishing and meaningful affiliation with the parents in her setting, and gives her a clear mandate to continue to work at creating opportunities to make relationships, with or without the aid of an open day.

Sandra – Challenges

Parental involvement with the setting and with their children's learning and development within the setting can be a challenge.

We try to encourage all of our families to take ownership and to become involved with the setting's policies and procedures. Getting to know the families that are part of our group is one of the most important factors of our job. We need to know the family culture to enable us to know the child.

We actively do this by continually inviting parents into the setting. Initially we do this when we are registering their child, we show them around and talk with them about our ethos, the EYFS and how the sessions are run. Most parents will take this opportunity to check out the building and get the feel of the pre-school. We also inform them that they are welcome to come into the setting at any time, that they can stay and play with their child during their settling-in time and also during their child's time with us. In my experience, most parents like to drop their child off and leave as quickly as possible. This is not always a bad thing – some children settle quickly after their parents have left, whilst some do not. When a child does not settle well, it means that a member of the team has to spend time consoling and comforting them, often on a one-to-one basis. The key person will talk to the parents and make suggestions of how we can work together to help settle the child into the routine of the setting. When parents work or have commitments whilst their child attends the setting, this can be difficult.

Parents have many reasons for not coming into the setting and taking time out to get to know us. Some work or attend university or college and this will often mean that they have to drop their child and rush. Some parents are shy or have a fear of authority; we need to break down these perceived barriers and try to gain the trust of all our families and this can only happen through good and varied communication such as: continual conversations, newsletters, posters and social media which keep parents and families up to date with what is going on within the setting, and by reminding them how we would like them to take part in their child's learning journey.

We are expected to have a baseline knowledge of a child as soon as they start at the pre-school, but we can only know a child when we get to know them and, therefore, we rely on parents and families for information. Parents can tell us how the child behaves in their home environment with known members of the family but some children react differently within a new environment with strangers.

Stay and play sessions are also organised, usually under the guise of a fundraiser, for example a coffee morning 'stay and play'. We feel that

(Continued)

(Continued)

parents and families might be more likely to attend if they are not on their own or pressured to be seen playing within the group. Parents might feel embarrassed to play amongst a group of children and adults when they are used to one to one with their child. Even with all of this effort some parents are still unwilling to engage fully. This can often make us as a team feel frustrated and sad to think that we are unable to convince parents that their involvement is so important to us.

My starting point is that parents do want the best care and education for their child and it is flattering that some will leave that totally to us as practitioners but it is our responsibility as professionals to remind them that they are their child's first educator and that we value their precious knowledge of their child. We do try to help them appreciate that we need their input so that we can plan for and support their child; we also ask for their contributions to their child's learning journey documents. Perhaps because trust is there and they know that they can approach any one of the team at any time they don't feel the need to do any more.

Parental involvement is a continual challenge for our setting but it is a challenge that we are committed to undertake.

The Interrelatedness of Principles and Action

Sue has a different method of reflection – using a visual map to help her see what is important in her setting; what she has and what she would like to have. The use of her jigsaw imagery is deliberate as it enables her to highlight the interrelatedness of all her thoughts, observations and plans and, in so doing, to make visible the importance of her work to develop the setting. As she says herself, looking at the overall puzzle that she created enabled her to see the actions that needed to take place, in what order, and that some needed to be tackled at the same time as each other in order to have maximum impact. Her observations would not have been so clear had she simply listed them. Her visual image could also be used in discussions with her staff; they would be able to see how she views the issue and, again, the impact of individual factors on each other, their connections and interdependency.

As Sue is new to the setting and unsure of the quality of the relationships she has made with a staff group who have been used to a very different leadership style (previously a directive manner rather than her democratic style), her visual reflective diagram is useful to communicate the idea of an underlying thinking about and creation of a forum for discussion and, ultimately, full ownership of the changes that need to happen in the setting. Sue's work shows the value of using visual methods to reflect or to engage in reflective activity. She has recorded her analysis and growing awareness of what she needs to do in writing as an additional layer of reflection, but she could have done this in visual form if she had wanted – adding labels; creating another tier to the jigsaw; maybe even changing to a weaving imagery that would show the different threads and how they interconnect to create a strong cloth (Pemberton, 2006; Whalley, 2006) – in itself a metaphor for what she is trying to achieve: a durable setting that is robust and resilient.

Sue then writes about her completed jigsaw and the intentions that inform it and are informed by it. In her reflection, we can see the structural and process aspects of quality coming together and the role of theory in helping her to develop an understanding of her practice. Yet despite the support of her team, along with the theory, the views of the parents are also important. It is not possible to know why parents do not want their children to get messy (maybe for practical reasons or due to ideas on how children should behave), but it does highlight once again that we work with competing discourses on what should happen within early years settings.

Sue – Challenge

I believe very strongly that outside play should be available to children every day and one of the challenges I was faced with when I first became manager of this new setting was how to ensure children had access to outside spaces when they wanted it. Under previous management the outside areas were only made available to the children at set times of the day and quite often only in fine weather. For me free-flow play is a better way of supporting children to pursue their own interests and so I wanted to establish it as soon as possible. In my previous setting we had a large outside space which children could access directly from the classroom and so free-flow play was easy to support. In my new setting accessing the outside space is rather more problematic. There are three areas in total with only two of them being accessible from the main building and only one of them directly from the classroom. The third area available to us is the church garden but it can only be accessed by taking the children out of the main premises.

(Continued)

(Continued)

I began my campaign for change by first seeking the opinions of the team and was pleased to discover that they were unanimously in favour of change but they were concerned about the reactions of the parents, some of whom did not like their children getting dirty. We decided to send out a letter explaining the changes being made and the reasons for doing this, quoting research evidence for the health benefits of outside play. I drew up a plan for how I thought we could best use the different areas to support the different groups of children and then we opened the doors and let the children go.

Almost immediately problems began to occur. The children loved having free access to the outside and for two weeks I do not think I saw a single child inside the building but the adults found this new way of working very stressful. We also had complaints from parents about the state of their children's clothes and we had complaints from members of the church because they now did not have free access to the back door to the church. It also became evident that the equipment for outside learning was not suitable for the children currently in the setting. I began to realise that my initial decision to open the doors when I did was based on incomplete information and that I needed to have a rethink.

In order to understand the problem more fully, I decided to look at each of the issues that had arisen as a single piece of a larger puzzle (Figure 6.1). By doing this, I began to see that one of the mistakes I had made was in approaching the task in a linear manner, one step at a time. By looking at the problem in terms of a puzzle I can now see that many of the issues are linked and therefore will need to be tackled simultaneously to get a more favourable outcome. Four themes began to emerge, the first of these being the need to think more carefully about how to meet the needs of the three groups of children: the 2-year-olds, the 3- and 4-year-olds, and the children with additional needs At the same time I will need to think about how to promote outside play with the parents and about how to ensure the children and adults are dressed appropriately for the weather. These two issues are clearly connected but also link to the issue of keeping the building warm whilst still keeping the outside accessible to the children. The third and fourth aspects that I need to think about are safety and resourcing. At the moment, free-flow play is on hold whilst we work through the issues I have highlighted above. The staff team is still fully on board with the idea, especially having seen the reaction of the children, but they are finding the lack of certainty quite challenging. I am hopeful that given time and support they will see that they too can be good dancers.

120 IMPLICATIONS FOR PRACTICE

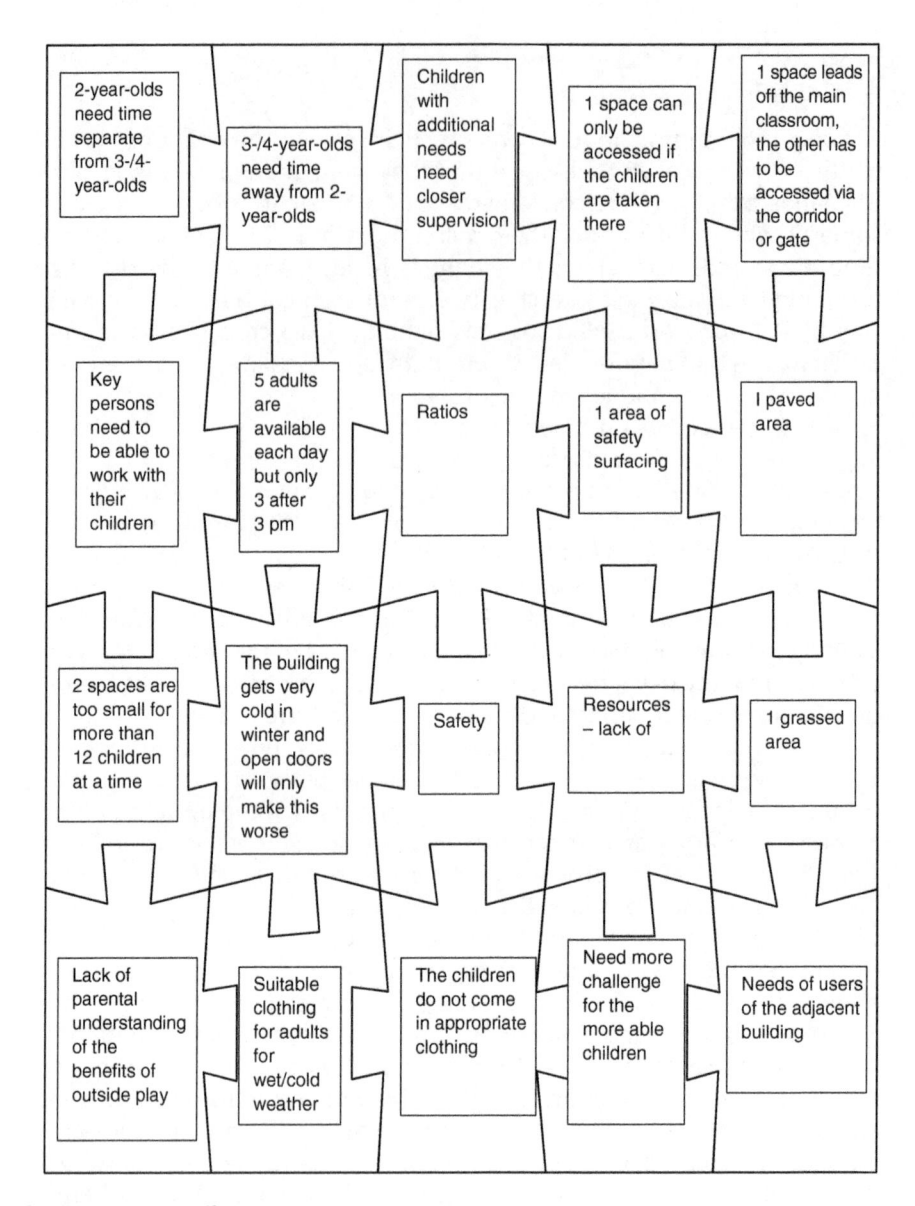

Figure 6.1 Sue's Jigsaw

Engaging the Team in Reflective Activity

Cheryl has introduced a particular reflective methodology into her setting that is now used by all her staff in order not only to reflect on the work they are doing, but also to share those reflections with each other to come to a mutual understanding and a shared commitment to improve practice. She has created a reflective ethos within her setting through the use of what she terms project books, which came about for a number of reasons – the challenge of introducing change; being beneficial for the children; and a meaningful way for her team to have ownership and understanding of these benefits, as well as providing an effective mechanism for continual reflection.

Leading from the front, Cheryl encourages her staff to engage in regular reflection on a whole series of topics: making children's learning visible; developing forest school principles; and so on. Cheryl demonstrates the value of the activity of team reflection where all are encouraged to offer comments that are shared through the use of the books. A dialogue is created that is asynchronous, which has great strength as it enables people to think about the responses they and others have made in order to come to a deep, well-considered and shared conclusion that is robust and open to scrutiny. It also reflects the social aspect of reflection that we referred to earlier in the chapter in drawing together the different views and perspectives of the team, acknowledging that we are all shaped by different understandings of early years, children and childhood. The books also provide a permanent record as well as being somewhere that is safe and respectful of the very vital journey towards the development of any particular aspect of the setting. Cheryl shows her awareness that by providing the project books, she is also creating confidence within her team and a detailed concept of ownership that can be articulated through all the work of the setting. This stance creates a collaborative ethos that is emotionally nurturing and facilitates creative practice. Cheryl is also an active participant in the reflective process, leading by example, and she shows this very clearly when she shares the work she has done with a colleague on sustained shared thinking. She also uses theory to inform her practice, especially the work of Freire (1970), and through his principle of informed action she encourages her staff to be flexible and creative in the work they do. As stated earlier, Cheryl is showing her awareness of the interplay between theory and practice and has put in place a mechanism by which her staff might embrace this perspective, improving their own use of theory in their work.

Cheryl – Challenge

In my setting one method of reflection is by using 'project books' to look at topics such as Schema, Forest School or Making Children's Learning Visible. By using peer observation and observations of the children, all

(Continued)

(Continued)

staff can contribute to the collaboration. The projects are a way of reflecting on working practice, what has gone well, how we can improve and why it will benefit the children. Over time it leads to an understanding and ownership of a shared approach to our working practice. Staff can develop a sense of belonging and confidence in what we do. As an example, in my setting we are influenced by Te Whariki strands and aspects when making observations of the children and using learning stories to record their development. We also recognise that risk is a context for learning and support 'risky play'. However, as a leader I need to support my team in implementing and feeling confident with this ethos.

The long-term aim is to create a whole-team vision with a clear purpose. Supervision and ongoing discussion mean constant reflection and revisiting of common goals and approaches such as our Rights Respecting aims and how we implement them with the children. Theory can develop our understanding, however it is putting it into practice and seeing the benefit that translate into meaningful practice, encouraging all members of staff to make their own connections and allowing time to apply them in a context that makes sense to them and leads to 'informed action' (Freire, 1970).

This is a dynamic approach where the practitioner can respond to children's needs and interests by adapting resources and working practice creatively and consistently using evidence-based theory to inform their actions. I was involved in a project on Sustained Shared Thinking with another member of staff. We videoed each other and then reflected on the recordings together. Although we were reaffirmed in much of what we saw and gained a deeper level of understanding of our interactions with the children, I feel one area that influenced us was the value of being quiet and observing as well as asking open-ended questions.

The impact of the environment and partnership with parents and other professionals will also reflect the quality of the setting. However, I would argue that a shared sense of purpose and expectation around pedagogical values, a commitment to continued professional development, and a culture of continually reflecting on the value and benefit to the children's learning and development are our starting point, and the biggest influence on quality.

Reflective Themes

Taking the opportunity to look at all four reflective accounts, noting the words that are used and the areas of focus, a number of significant themes can be discerned:

1. All four accounts demonstrate the central importance of the children in their settings and how all the planning and activity are centred on consideration of the care and education of each individual child. The well-being of children is privileged in the accounts of our case studies, despite what has been outlined in earlier chapters regarding the managerialist rhetoric of policy. In regard to leadership, our case study practitioners do not reflect the autocratic managerial models that have been favoured in recent policy and equally they do not uphold the modernist approach to quality that favours an approach of managing children as a project to get right. Our practitioners are aware of, but not bound by, a view of child development as a universal process and are resisting the current impetus to make curriculum planning a narrow and outcome-driven procedure with high degrees of predictability (Brooker, 2014).
2. Relationships and the engagement that they promote is an important aspect of these accounts. Engagement with families is seen as crucial to the well-being of the child and the setting, demonstrating that these leaders have paid regard to the expectations of policy makers and the research that shows how important parental involvement is to a child's successful development. As we have said, there are some aspects of the discursive production of early years practice that can feel appropriate and helpful. However, it is interesting to note that there is a very practical edge to the voices of these leaders; they know what works in their relationship with parents and they know what matters – the relationship itself and their energies are focused on getting that right rather than simply complying with a policy directive.
3. The relationship that leaders enjoy with their staff team is also an important aspect of determining the quality of the setting, generating a significant leadership task that they all take seriously. There is recognition of the importance of developing an ethos of collaborative process – learning and developing together; and an active engagement in the process that gives a clear message on the prominent positioning of positive, nurturing relationships in every aspect of the setting. Sue's jigsaw shows the effort and thought that has gone into communicating her ideas and the rationale behind them in a way that enables her staff to follow her thought processes and take ownership of her vision of how the outdoor space might be improved. Cheryl shows a strong commitment to developing a reflective environment where all team members are involved together in developing their capacity to reflect on their work and improve their setting. Underpinning all the work here is a good understanding as to the amount of emotional labour that is involved in working with children and families. All four want their workers to engage with the

children and families at a deep emotional level and see their role as providing the ethos and support to sustain that activity.
4. Following on from the development of effective relationships with the staff team is the strong thread that runs throughout all of the accounts of the principles of transformational leadership – the creation and development of a clear vision of the service they provide which has a strong value base and is clearly articulated through their work. There is a commitment to finding ways of developing common goals that are articulated through a shared sense of purpose and the facility for all in the staff team to gain ownership of the principles of practice and any vision of how the setting might be. All four refer to the close-knit communities they lead and how they have developed those dialogues and relationships. Sue and Cheryl have both sought collaboration with their staff teams, but have gone about this in very different ways. Sue, being new to her setting, demonstrates mindfulness of her need to get her staff on board with her ideas and uses her jigsaw reflection to identify what she feels are the key issues. She writes vividly of her realisation that she cannot simply import an idea, however principled, from a previous setting, and that she has to start by having discussions with the team. She has to encourage a collaborative culture of working together and then look at how they might, together, realise the full potential of the setting. Cheryl starts with a collegiate philosophy by using a group approach to reflection that enables reflective dialogue and challenge to take place in a spirit of co-construction and trust. Jacky and Sandra show their efforts to understand what is happening within their settings so that they might better support their staff with their work.
5. The four accounts show clearly the powerful impact that engaging in reflective activity has had on their capacity to lead high quality provision. We see different methods being used, even in this small snapshot: visual imagery; project books and writing techniques, either as a free-flow stream of consciousness (James, 1892) or through the use of a model such as that promoted by Schön (1983) to systematically guide and encourage deep thought.

However, Jacky provides us with a very useful note of caution when she articulates the danger of being introspective. Her deep commitment to her setting, her children and her staff lead her, through reflection, to question her skills and make her begin to doubt herself. Elliott and Coker (2008) illustrate clearly the danger of self-reflection to negatively affect a person's sense of well-being and happiness, especially if they were not feeling happy or confident when they embarked on the process.

Any reflective process should be carefully supported by good knowledge of the self and the culture within the setting or by an effective supervision/appraisal framework in the workplace.

> **Jacky – The Reflection Process**
>
> Reflective practice is a personally challenging process which can lead you to be over-critical of your work. Because I care about the quality of my practice and the impact this has on the children, my concerns began to impact on my positive attitude, leading me to question my practitioner skills. It was in fact my skills and experience as a practitioner that led me to act in the most appropriate way for the 'storming' stage – maintaining a consistent approach and reminding the children what is expected.

Jacky shows her use of self-knowledge to mediate her downward spiral – she reminds herself that she is capable of meeting the challenge, that she has done so before and that it will work. This is what Ghaye and Ghaye (1998: 3) define as 'practice with principle': 'Being professionally self-critical without being destructive and overly negative.' Thus, reflection should be a positive experience, enabling practitioners to 'feel' their work. Johns (2009) argues that reflection should be empowering, enabling practitioners to develop insight into their practice and work towards more rewarding ways of working and allowing an authoritative, assertive and political voice to emerge.

Why Would You Not Want Reflective Leaders?

The work in this chapter has shown the power of reflective activity. Reflective practice has enabled these four leaders to mediate and adapt statutory frameworks and policy directives to develop creative and responsive practice for their settings in their communities. They have articulated the unique natures of their settings, their children and families and their staff and lead high quality provision as a consequence. What these four accounts show is that reflective activity should not be regarded as an optional extra, to be engaged in if there is time, or to be dismissed as an indulgence or luxury. They show very clearly that it should be a way of being; a deeply embedded facet of the culture or ethos of a setting in which the examination of all actions from the routine and mundane to the extraordinary and unusual sheds light on the nuances, subtleties and significances, and encourages staff to use that knowledge to develop practice. We return to the question heading this section and ask again – why would you not want reflective leaders, given all the rich creativity that reflection unlocks, the emotional nourishment that it offers and the quality of interaction, planning and creativity that it facilitates?

Chapter Summary

In this chapter we have considered how reflection can help you to think about your practice in regards to the context that you are in – the children, families and colleagues that you work with. We have looked at the powerful role that engaging in reflective practice has in supporting practitioners in their attempts to understand the impact of their personal views and beliefs on their practice and what and who has informed the development of those perspectives. We have demonstrated that there are numerous ways to reflect on practice; it is a matter of personal choice as to what works best, enabling a detailed exploration of a wide range of issues relevant to early years practice from how the position of the child in the setting is articulated in practice, to the importance and relevance of developing sustaining relationships with children, families colleagues and communities in daily early years practice.

Further Reading

Hughes, S. (2009) 'Leadership, management and sculpture: how arts-based activities can transform learning and deepen understanding', *Reflective Practice: International and Multidisciplinary Perspectives*, 109 (1): 77–90.

Hughes' article is focused on a Masters in Leadership and Management, using art to explore the thoughts and feelings of participants. He observes the use of metaphor in their work and the way the activities 'free up' the participants to explore and make explicit their hidden, implicit drivers.

Mason, J. (2002) *Researching Your Own Practice: The Discipline of Noticing.* London: RoutledgeFalmer.

This is an inspiring book, encouraging us to notice what goes on around us, taking time to explore that which we take for granted. This perspective is really important to those who are starting to be reflective; all too often, we think that we should be looking at the unusual or key events that occur around us. Mason reminds us of the richness of learning that is situated in the mundane.

CONCLUSION

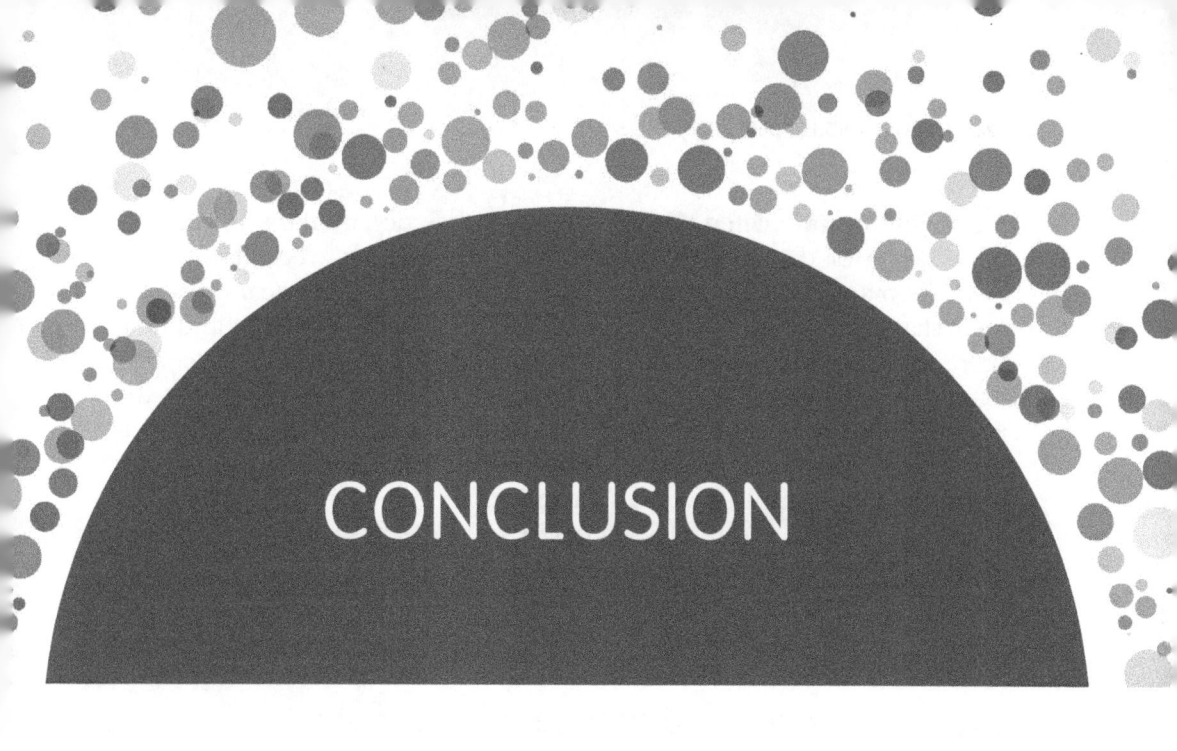

> **Chapter Overview**
>
> In this final chapter, we look back at the contents of the book and clarify the main arguments that have emerged and which require highlighting with further discussion. We take a further look at the two key themes that have run through this book: the external forces that look to shape our understandings of quality and leadership, and how leaders seek to respond to the needs and requirements of their local communities. Finally, we return to our central debate on how creative leaders can develop their own understanding of leadership and quality and use that knowledge to enhance the experience of all those who access their services.

We do not dispute the importance of quality and leadership, but we hope that we have demonstrated in this book that there is more than one interpretation of those terms and how they interrelate. Throughout this book, we have offered debate on the different understandings of quality and leadership that exist and we have explored their appeal. There are many more possibilities that we have not explored or that have not yet been identified, and the discourse on what constitute leadership and quality will and should continue to be a lively discussion in order that new information and new ways of looking at things can be developed, as well as old ideas and ways of working being held up to scrutiny.

Chapters 5 and 6 demonstrate clearly the effort engaged in by creative leaders to construct their own understandings of these terms and how they might be articulated through the work they do and the services they offer. Some of the main influences on that essential work have come from the many stakeholders who have an interest in early years services, their shape and form. For many stakeholders, such as parents and children, there are deeply personal reasons for being involved and seeking to shape the identity and core offer of early years services. For others, the interest is more political with global considerations of wealth generation and international development underpinned by drivers of economic value and the careful use of tax payers' money. In this final chapter, we explore how both economic and emotional aspects shape the quality of early years provision and the role of the leader in mediating between these often competing discourses.

External Forces on Understandings of the Early Years

In considering our two key themes of top-down and bottom-up pressures on leading quality early years provision that we explore later in this chapter, there are a number of other interrelated topics that have emerged as important issues for examination in this book. The first has been our exploration of the implications of modernist and post-structuralist approaches to both quality and leadership. We would argue that the inclination towards a modernist approach espoused by many policy-making bodies, whilst having the potential for developing a secure, predictable world, can have the effect of discouraging a more creative attitude to the task of leading a setting of high calibre and may inhibit a disposition to be responsive to the needs of the local community. We would advocate that a post-structuralist approach enables leaders and practitioners to examine and thereby deconstruct their understandings of what constitutes a quality environment for young children and their families and begin to reconstruct a new understanding that has legitimacy for their work in the community. We will be returning to this sense of deconstruction and reconstruction throughout this chapter, as it is such an important and exhilarating aspect of the leadership task.

In identifying the role of deconstruction to better understand who and what is shaping understandings of quality and leadership in the early years, we would also like to take a moment to pause and reflect on how post-structuralism (and the notion of deconstruction) has become a prevailing discourse in the early years. As we have outlined, discourses represent a way of thinking about talking about a given topic. In recent years, post-structuralism has become a way to speak about early years services. As mentioned, this is in response to modernist agendas in an attempt to highlight that the world is not as predictable (or prescriptive) as modernism would presume. We feel that post-structuralism has a lot to offer in enabling alternative ways of approaching quality and leadership in the early years, particularly in resisting attempts for quality and leadership to become about standardisation and conformity. Post-structuralism embraces uncertainty and fluidity in understandings of quality and leadership, but we return to what we considered in Chapters 5 and 6 – that the deconstruction process does not have to be a rejection of everything that we once held to be 'true' about early years provision. For us, post-structuralism is about creating a deeper understanding of why we do what we do. We do not want it to be a governing discourse that states how early years services should be talked about, rather it is one that can facilitate thinking.

Another significant topic that has been highlighted throughout this book is the rise in popularity of key theoretical perspectives such as human capital theory in the development of policy initiatives and the growth of early years services. Human capital theory has dominated recent discourse on the development of early years services and its inherent concept of investment has promoted a world view of children as a project to be 'got right' and, consequently, the idea that their future is more important than their present. Indeed, the discourse of many influential documents from both supranational and national organisations has displayed an overt inclination to have a particular focus on a child's academic achievement and their opportunity to contribute to economic life once they reach adulthood. Whilst evident internationally, it is clear that at national level there are different interpretations and levels of emphasis on a child's academic achievement, such as it being offset by a recognition of the child's holistic well-being as well. In our own context, the (re)creation of the EYFS and its concomitant assessment processes, concentrating on a child's readiness for school and formal learning through Ofsted inspectorate assessments and narratives, see a focus on estimations of children's future capacity as members of the workforce and tax payers. Such a concentration on building a strong foundation for future learning has promoted a focus on highly predictable variables which, in turn, has led to the development of an inspection process that privileges measurable aspects of quality, with the consequence that the less measurable, such as the emotional features of a setting, are less noticed or totally absent.

We have other concerns surrounding the prevailing human capital discourse in the early years. It is indisputable that a human capitalist view of children has underpinned the long overdue increase in provision for young children below school age. It is also true that an increase in provision should be welcomed as it gives families the vital support services they need and greater choice of where those services might be obtained, and offers children more opportunities for the play and social engagement that promote their natural inclination to investigate, explore and experiment in the world that is laid out before them. What is not so welcome is the deficit model that seems to have followed in its wake; the assumption that good things will not happen in these settings unless there are strict expectations on the staff and leaders which are rigorously inspected by a central, government-supported agency utilising the panoptic surveillance discussed in Chapter 1. Furthermore, an exacting and narrow emotionology has been able to develop that places clear expectations on the display of emotional engagement between practitioners and children under the guise of professionalising the workforce, as discussed in Chapter 4. It would seem that whilst we should celebrate the focus on early years services with the evidence of enhanced availability and greater choice, we should also be concerned about the less commented on risks of commodification and homogenisation that can clearly be seen as a theme running through the current view of early years services as playing a major role in 'fixing' children.

Further, what we have noticed as we take this opportunity to review our work is the high use we have made of the word 'different' – in a world that seems to wish to commodify childcare, to remove difference and replace it with homogeneity and predictability, our choice of words would seem contradictory and inflammatory. However, we feel its use is apposite; we would encourage practitioners not only to celebrate difference in its diverse forms, but to also actively seek it out through their constructions of what leadership and quality mean for them as individuals and for them as part of very different, vibrant communities. The work focused on in Chapters 5 and 6 highlights the capacity of leaders to be playful with difference, to buck the trend of predictability and enjoy their relationship with each child who uses their service.

Finally, in this section, we wish to acknowledge our frequent use of the word 'good'. Indeed, we raised the question of what we mean by 'good' in our introduction, as we recognised that there was something to debate in the use of this common word which often goes overlooked, regarding it simply as a useful adjective. A brief search in any dictionary will show a wide variation in its meaning and its use (www.thesaurus.com/browse/good). It might mean pleasant, virtuous, competent, useful, considerable, reliable, authentic or well behaved. We would suggest that there are debates still to be had as to which of these meanings are being applied and by whom as a mechanism for understanding the different perspectives of those engaged in the debate. Some might regard a 'good' setting as a well-behaved setting; a 'good' leader as being a competent leader; and 'good' quality as meaning reliable, and, by using such definitions, the question should be asked – what are the implications? The underpinning assumptions when the word 'good' is used are therefore worthy of debate as they will have made a serious contribution to the construction of early years services. For example, a view of 'good' leadership as 'well behaved' might imply an expectation of compliance, giving justification for inspection and regulatory systems that make judgements about the compliance rather than the service. We would propose the use of good to mean authentic in terms of leadership as it would seem that authentic leaders are the most resilient and offer an individual rather than a homogenous service. In terms of quality, 'good' meaning reliable would seem to be useful, implying a sustained state of affairs that parents, children and other stakeholders can trust with confidence.

How Might Settings Respond to the Communities in Which They are Located?

There has been a great deal written about the sensitivities of very young children to the emotional climate of the environment they inhabit (for example, Dahlberg et al., 2013; Elfer and Dearnley, 2007; Jones and Pound, 2008) and therefore about the importance of developing the right milieu in which children can feel genuinely cared for. In Chapters 5 and 6, we saw the actions of four dedicated leaders working hard to create and sustain the best environment for the children and families they serve. More globally, we have also seen the emergence of a strict professional emotionology that may inhibit the expression of genuine emotional care between children and practitioners. Thus, it is clear that leaders have a number of tensions to navigate and some may feel that this is an impossible task. There would seem to be a number of ways in which leaders can effectively respond to the needs of their communities whilst navigating the choppy waters of requirements, expectations and surveillance. One of these is through education and training, using theoretical knowledge and practical experience to inform decision making and thus ensure a solid platform for the development of the service. Chapters 5 and 6 explored the value of knowledge in all its forms and the confidence that it gives leaders to enable decisions to be made. There has been a substantial expansion in the education programmes available for practitioners as this has been regarded as a key factor in improving the quality of provision (Payler and Georgeson, 2014). However, Georgeson and Payler note, with concern, the limited representation of men, people with disabilities and people from black minority ethnic backgrounds in the early years workforce, which leads to questions about the suitability of the training and education on offer. The increased emphasis on a graduate workforce adds a further layer of learning opportunity for people wanting to work with young children, but requires significant outlay and commitment from participants who are then looking at work with low levels of pay and job security, particularly when compared with teachers, health professionals and social workers. Education is important – knowing not only how something works but why and how it might be enhanced and developed is invaluable and should be encouraged and promoted across the workforce. Critical thinking, using that knowledge critically, thoughtfully and reflectively, should also be encouraged. As shown in Chapter 6, developing the facility to reflect on and hold up to scrutiny what is done, why and with what consequences enables a practitioner to move from being technically able – knowing *what* to do and *when* to do it – to being a professional – knowing *why* it is done and *how* it might be done differently or better, responding to local, immediate conditions or any changes that might occur at any time. The provision and leadership of quality early years services has moved a long way from the community groups of women providing care in support of other women that we identified in Chapter 3. Early years provision has a rich history of theory that informs and shapes early years practice, but does so in conjunction with other important forms of knowledge.

Experience is invaluable to practitioners and leaders, especially in terms of adding another layer of practical confidence to that created through the acquisition of theoretical knowledge. Students undertaking placements, a career structure that enables learning from the bottom up and an effective supervision and appraisal system are all mechanisms by which early years workers might gain experience and develop expertise. Yet experience is more than just spending time working with children to help guide you in the practicalities of working in a busy early years setting. Experience is also about an appreciation of how your own life history shapes and informs your understanding of quality and leadership and how your experiences of knowing and understanding the children and families that you work with are important forms of knowledge that combine with theoretical knowledge to guide and develop your practice. We feel that the combination of different forms of knowledge to guide practice is exemplified in developments in the sociology of childhood. As an early years practitioner, listening to the voice of the child and supporting their autonomous learning are part of an appreciation of the excitement and joy that can come from seeing a child explore their world, only now there is pedagogical theory that explains this natural exploration in relation to child development, and a sociology of childhood that explains what has long been practised – children being part of our society.

Reflective engagement creates an opportunity to make links between theory and practice, bringing together the various forms of knowledge that we hold. In its turn, reflection helps to develop an awareness of self that enhances personal confidence and efficacy. Developing into a thoughtful early years practitioner and/or leader through learning, experience and reflection offers the opportunity to improve personal resilience and cultivate strategies to cope with the strictures of the landscape of modern early years service provision. Rodd (2006) talks about the requirement on leaders to lead the way in challenging policy times, to be advocates for the children and families they care for, and this is best achieved through the confidence given by knowledge, experience and personal reflection.

Of course, not everyone is going to be an effective leader of an early years setting, no matter how much learning is engaged in – those with a personal disposition to work with children and families, to lead others through the boggy landscape of EYFS, Ofsted and a myriad of other expectations, will be the ones most likely to succeed. The leadership literature has moved on from trait theory as a predominant approach, but the sense of what qualities make a good leader is enduring. Those people who have a strong ethic of care, who are able to communicate with others, able to maintain their personal authenticity and therefore integrity, are those who would be the most successful as leaders of strong, responsive, quality early years settings. We can therefore see that the link between quality and leadership is that they are integral; the development of a culture of quality within a setting is the responsibility of the leader (Leeson et al., 2012), who in turn must be a confident, motivated individual with integrity and in possession of a number of qualities already highlighted and discussed. How far that leader is able to lead effectively, given the pressure from external drivers and stakeholders, is an individual conundrum that can be addressed through the use of a bricolage approach: deconstruct the discourses, expectations, guidelines and policies that surround you and, through that process, begin to construct your own theory of what constitutes quality in your setting and of how best to lead your team to support your children and families.

Throughout this book, we have emphasised that we do not hold the answer to what it means to lead quality early years services. Rather, we have considered how you can navigate your way between the various external pressures that shape and inform how quality and leadership in the early years are understood. Thus, we have considered that there are many forms of quality and leadership – what is important is finding an approach that is meaningful to you and the context that you work in. What we have aimed to do in this book is to support you in considering what and who have shaped your understanding of quality and leadership so that you can articulate that understanding, and we hope that we have given you plenty to think about and to guide those processes. As we noted in our Introduction, we can often feel constrained or bogged down by imposed understandings of both quality and leadership, but we hope you have found that they are in fact liberating terms – it just depends on how you look at them.

GLOSSARY

Term	Overview
Accountability	Accountability requires a person or an institution to be answerable for their actions, decisions or comments. Explicit accountability asks that the level of answerability is open and transparent, understood by all rather than assumed or implied.
Discourse	Discourse represents a way of viewing, thinking and speaking about the social world. The way of speaking and thinking looks to normalise behaviour. The normalisation process means that bias and subjectivities become hidden. In the example of politics, discourses conceal assumptions and render political objectives and ideologies invisible.
Educare	Educare represents the combining of education and childcare to represent those who work in early years services as concerned with both the education and care of young children.
Emotionology	Emotionology explores the links between our thoughts and our emotions and how that linking informs or drives our subsequent behaviour.
Human capital theory	Human capital is an economic theory that represents how education is an investment in an individual's knowledge, skills and other attributes. The knowledge, skills and other attributes are embodied and can be utilised in labour (paid employment) for economic gain.
Managerialism	Managerialism has become a global term for hierarchical and measurable decision-making processes that produce outcomes with a lack of consideration as to the impact on or implications for the individuals concerned. It is argued that managerialism is one-dimensional, anti-democratic and authoritarian (Klikauer, 2013).
Modernity	Modernity reflects a period in history, but also a set of socio-cultural norms that privilege a rational, objective, empirical (scientific) view of the world. Social life is regarded as structural and ordered.

(Continued)

(Continued)

Term	Overview
Neo-liberal government	Neo-liberal governments are those that have moved away from a system of the state (the government) providing services to a system of a free-market economy. Under a free-market economy, privatisation is favoured as a means for governments to reduce the level of monies they are required to spend on services.
Panoptic gaze	The panoptic gaze represents the notion of an overseer (e.g. an individual, organisation or government) who looks to control and monitor social life. The gaze acts as a form of social control whereby individuals conform as they feel as if they are being watched.
Paradigm	A paradigm is an agreed world view, underlying theory(ies); it is an understanding of how something might be regarded.
Post-structuralism	Post-structuralism challenges the notion of the rational and coherent knowledge that is present in modernist approaches. It is a critical theory that highlights the complexities of human life rather than assume that it is rational and structural, as per modernity.
Process quality	Process quality relates to the experience of the child, such as adult–child interactions, parent relationships, the learning experiences of children, etc.
Social agency	Social agency is the ability of individuals to make free choices. It is the ability to act on one's will. However, many structural features in society such as social class, age and gender can all limit how free an individual's choice is.
Social investment	Broadly speaking, social investment is about investing in people. Governments seek to invest economic monies to achieve predetermined economic and social goals. Examples include education and health care.
Structural quality	Structural features of quality relate to things such as ratios, qualification levels of staff, furniture, square footage required for each child, etc. and are often regarded as those features that can be measured.
Supranational organisation	Supranational refers to those organisations whose scope extends beyond any one country. Examples include the World Bank, the OECD, Unicef and the EU. There are variations in the function of different supranational organisations, but in essence they look to secure international co-operation between countries.

REFERENCES

Adair, J. (1973) *Action-Centred Leadership*. London: McGraw-Hill.
Adams, S., Alexander, E., Drummond, M. J. and Moyles, J. (2004) *Inside the Foundation Stage: Recreating the Reception Year*. London: Association of Teachers and Lecturers. Available at: www.atl.org.uk/Images/Inside%20 the%20foundation%20stage.pdf (accessed 30 April 2015).
Ancona, D., Malone, T. W., Orlikowski, W. J. and Senge, P. M. (2007) 'In praise of the incomplete leader', *Harvard Business Review*, (February), pp. 99–102 (www.hbr.org).
Attard, K. (2008) 'Uncertainty for the reflective practitioner: a blessing in disguise', *Reflective Practice*, 9 (3): 307–17.
Aubrey, C. (2007) *Leading and Managing in the Early Years*. London: SAGE.
Avolio, B. J. and Gardner, W. L. (2005) 'Authentic leadership development: getting to the roots of positive forms of leadership', *Leadership Quarterly*, 16: 315–38.
Baker, S. (2007) 'Followership: the theoretical foundation of a contemporary construct', *Journal of Leadership and Organizational Studies*, 14 (1): 50–60.
Ball, S. J. (2008) *The Education Debate*. Bristol: Policy Press.
Begley, P. (2001) 'In pursuit of authentic school leadership practices', *International Journal of Leadership in Education*, 4 (4): 353–65.
Bennett, J. (2006) 'New policy conclusions from starting strong II: an update on the OECD early childhood policy reviews', *European Early Childhood Education Research Journal*, 14 (2): 141–56.
Bernstein, P. (1996) *Against the Gods: The Remarkable Story of Risk*. Chichester: Wiley.
Bertram, T. and Pascal, C. (2014) *Early Years Literature Review*. Birmingham: Centre for Research in Early Childhood (CREC) (www.crec.co.uk).
Blackmore, J. (1995) 'Policy as dialogue: feminist administrators working for educational change', *Gender and Education*, 7 (3): 293–313.
Blake, R. and Moulton, J. (1964) *The Managerial Grid*. London: Bloomsbury.
Blundell, R. and Lockett, N. (2011) *Exploring Entrepreneurship: Practices and Perspectives*. Oxford: Oxford University Press.
Boag-Munroe, G. (2014) 'Parents as partners: the new politics of parenting', in J. Moyles, J. Payler and J. Georgeson (eds), *Early Years Foundations: Critical Issues*. Maidenhead: Open University Press, pp. 155–65.

Bolden, R., Hawkins, B., Gosling, J. and Taylor, S. (2011) *Exploring Leadership: Individual, Organisational and Societal Perspectives*. Oxford: Oxford University Press.

Bolton, B. and Thompson, J. (2004) *Entrepreneurs: Talent, Temperament, Technique* (2nd edition). Oxford: Butterworth-Heinemann.

Bourdieu, P. (1992) *Invitation to a Reflexive Sociology*. Chicago, IL: University of Chicago Press.

Brayfield, A. and Korintus, M. (2011) 'Early childhood socialization: societal context and childrearing values in Hungary', *Journal of Early Childhood Research*, 9 (3): 262–79.

Bronfenbrenner, U. (1979) *The Ecology of Human Development: Experiments by Nature and Design*. Cambridge, MA: Harvard University Press.

Brooker, L. (2014) 'An overview of education in England', in J. Moyles, J. Payler and J. Georgeson (eds), *Early Years Foundations: Critical Issues*. London: Open University Press, pp. 6–16.

Burns, J. (1978) *Leadership*. New York: Harper & Row.

Calder, P., Leeson, C., Wild, M., Needham, M., Nightingale, B., Barron, I. and Silberfeld, C. (2013) *More Great Childcare: Interrogating Values and Assumptions in Recent Documentation Relating to Children's Day Care*. Symposium presentation at EECERA, September, Tallinn, Estonia.

Callender, C. (2000) *The Barriers to Childcare Provision*. London: Department for Education and Employment (DfEE).

Cameron, C. (2006) 'Men in the nursery revisited: issues of male workers and professionalism', *Contemporary Issues in Early Childhood*, 7 (1): 68–79.

Campbell, C. (2011) *How to Involve Hard-to-Reach Parents: Encouraging Meaningful Parental Involvement with Schools*. Nottingham: National College for School Leadership (NCSL).

Campbell-Barr, V. (2009a) 'Care and business orientations in the delivery of childcare: an exploratory study', *Journal of Early Childhood Research*, 7 (1): 76–93.

Campbell-Barr, V. (2009b) 'Contextual issues in assessing value for money in early years education', *National Institute Economic Review*, 207 (1): 90–101.

Campbell-Barr, V. (2012) 'Early years education and the value for money folklore', *European Early Childhood Education Research Journal*, 20 (3): 423–37.

Campbell-Barr, V. (2014) 'Constructions of early childhood education and care provision: negotiating discourses', *Contemporary Issues in Early Childhood*, 15 (1): 5–17.

Campbell-Barr, V. (2015) 'The research, policy and practice triangle in early childhood education and care', in R. Parker-Rees and C. Leeson (eds), *Early Childhood Studies: An Introduction to the Study of Children's Worlds and Children's Lives* (4th edition). London: SAGE, pp. 163–78.

Campbell-Barr, V. and Nygård, M. (2014) 'Losing sight of the child? Human capital theory and its role for early childhood education and care policies in Finland and England since the mid-1990s', *Contemporary Issues in Early Childhood*, 15 (4): 346–59.

Campbell-Barr, V., Lavelle, M. and Wickett, K. (2011) 'Exploring alternative approaches to child outcome assessments in Children's Centres', *Early Child Development and Care*, 182 (7): 859–74.

Carter Dillon, R. (2013) 'A critique of euro-centric perspectives on early childhood education and care in the Gambia', in J. Georgeson and J. Payler (eds), *International Perspectives on Early Childhood Education and Care*. Maidenhead: Open University Press, pp. 53–63.

Case, P., Case, S. and Catling, S. (2000) '"Please show you're working": a critical assessment of the impact of OFSTED inspection on primary teachers', *British Journal of Sociology of Education*, 21 (4): 605–21.

Cattell, R. B. (1966) *The Scientific Analysis of Personality*. Chicago, IL: Aldine.

Catton, S., Crawford, C. and Dearden, L. (2014) *The Economic Consequences for Pre-school Education and Quality*. London: Institute of Fiscal Studies.

Champy, J. (2009) 'Authentic leadership', *Executive Forum*, 54: 39–44.

Children's Workforce Development Council (CWDC) (2006) *Early Years Professional National Standards*. Leeds: CWDC.

Clark, A. and Moss, P. (2011) *Listening to Young Children: The Mosaic Approach* (2nd edition). London: National Children's Bureau.

Clarke, J., Smith, N. and Vidler, E. (2005) 'Consumerism and the reform of public services: inequalities and instabilities', in M. Powell, L. Baud and K. Clarke (eds), *Social Policy Review 17: Analysis and Debate in Social Policy*. Bristol: Policy Press, pp. 167–82.

Cleveland, G., Forer, B., Hyatt, D., Japel, C. and Krashinsky, M. (2007) *An Economic Perspective on the Current and Future Role of Nonprofit Provision of Early Learning and Child Care Services in Canada: Final Project Report*. Toronto: University of Toronto.

Coleyshaw, J., Whitmarsh, J., Jopling, M. and Hadfield, M. (2012) *An Exploration of Progress, Leadership and Impact, as a Part of the Longitudinal Study of Early Years Professional Status*. Wolverhampton: University of Wolverhampton.

Cottle, M. and Alexander, E. (2012) 'Quality in early years settings: government, research and practitioners' perspectives', *British Educational Research Journal*, 38 (4): 635–54.

Crawford, M. (2014) *Developing as an Educational Leader*. London: SAGE.

Cunha, M. (2005) *Bricolage in Organizations*. Faculdade de Economia da Universidade Nova de Lisboa (FEUNL), Working Paper No. 474. Available at: http://dx.doi.org/10.2139/ssrn.882784 (accessed 12 February 2015).

Curtis, L. and Burton, D. (2009) 'Naïve change agent or canny political collaborator? The change in leadership role from nursery school to Children's Centre', *Education*, 3: 287–99.

Dahlberg, G. and Moss, P. (2005) *Ethics and Politics in Early Childhood Education*. London: RoutledgeFalmer.

Dahlberg, G., Moss, P. and Pence, A. (2013) *Beyond Quality in Early Childhood Education and Care: Languages of Evaluation*. London: Routledge.

Dalea, R. and Robertson, S. (2004) 'Interview with Boaventura de Sousa Santos', *Globalisation, Societies and Education*, 2 (2): 147–60.

Davis, G. (2012) 'A documentary analysis of the use of leadership and change theory in changing practice in early years settings', *Early Years: An International Research Journal*, 32 (3): 266–76.

Daycare Trust (2010) *Childcare Costs Survey 2010*. London: Daycare Trust.

Department for Children, Schools and Families (DCSF) (2008) *The Impact of Parental Involvement on Children's Education*. Nottingham: DCSF.

Department for Education (DfE) (2013) *More Great Childcare*. London: Department for Education.

Department for Education (DfE) (2014) *Statutory Framework for the Early Years Foundation Stage Setting the Standards for Learning, Development and Care for Children from Birth to Five*. London: Department for Education.

Department for Education and Employment (DfEE) (1998) *Meeting the Childcare Challenge: A Framework and Consultation Document*. London: Crown.

Department for Education and Skills (DfES) (2004) *Every Child Matters: Change for Children*. London: HM Government.

Douglass, A. and Gittell, J. (2012) 'Transforming professionalism: relational bureaucracy and parent–teacher partnerships in child care settings', *Journal of Early Childhood Research*, 10 (3): 267–81.

Dunlop, A.-W. (2008) *A Literature Review on Leadership in the Early Years*. Available at: www.educationscotland.gov.uk/resources/a/leadershipreview.asp (accessed 10 November 2014).

Earley, P. and Weindling, D. (2004) *Understanding School Leadership*. London: SAGE.

Ebbeck, M. and Waniganayake, M. (2003) *Early Childhood Professionals: Leading Today and Tomorrow*. Sydney: MacLennan & Petty.

Ehren, M. and Visscher, A. (2006) 'Towards a theory on the impact of school inspections', *British Journal of Education Studies*, 54 (1): 51–72.

Eisenstadt, N., Sylva, K., Mathers, S. and Taggart, B. (2013) *More Great Childcare: Research Evidence*. Oxford/London: University of Oxford and Institute of Education. Available at: www.ecersuk.org/resources/More+Great+Childcare+Research+Evidence+March+2013.pdf (accessed 1 May 2015).

Elfer, P. and Dearnley, K. (2007) 'Nurseries and emotional well-being: evaluating an emotionally containing model of continuing professional development', *Early Years: An International Journal of Research and Development*, 27 (3): 267–79.

Elliott, I. and Coker, C. (2008) 'Independent self-construal, self-reflection, and self-rumination: a path model for predicting happiness', *Australian Journal of Psychology*, 60 (3): 127–34.

Ellison, G., Barker, A. and Kulasuriya, T. (2009) *Work and Care: A Study of Modern Parents*. London: Equality and Human Rights Committee.

Eraut, M. (2000) 'Non-formal learning and tacit knowledge in professional work', *British Journal of Educational Psychology*, 70 (1): 113–36.

Evangelou, M., Sylva, K., Kyriacou, M., Wild, M. and Glenny, G. (2009) *Early Years Learning and Development: A Literature Review* (Research Report No. DCSF-RR176). London: Department for Children, Schools and Families (DCSF) Publications.

Fenech, M. (2011) 'An analysis of the conceptualisation of "quality" in early childhood education and care empirical research: promoting "blind spots" as foci for future research', *Contemporary Issues in Early Childhood*, (2): 102–17.

Fiedler, F. E. and Chemers, M. M. (1974) *Leadership and Effective Management*. Glenview, IL: Scott, Foresman & Co.

Fleer, M. (2003) 'Early childhood education as an evolving "community of practice" or as lived "social reproduction": researching the "taken-for-granted"', *Contemporary Issues in Early Childhood*, 4 (1): 64–79.

Foucault, M. (1995) *Discipline and Punish: The Birth of the Prison*. New York: Second Vintage Books:

Freidman, J. and Sturdy, J. (2011) 'The influence of economic crisis on early childhood development: a review of pathways and measured impact', in H. Alderman (ed.), *No Small Matter: The Impact of Poverty, Shocks, and Human Capital Investments in Early Childhood Development*. Washington, DC: World Bank, pp. 51–84.

Freire, P. (1970) *Pedagogy of the Oppressed*. New York: Herder & Herder.

Freud, S. (1917) *Mourning and Melancholia*. In The Standard Edition of the Complete Psychological Works of Sigmund Freud, Volume XIV (1914–1916): On the History of the Psycho-Analytic Movement, Papers on Metapsychology and Other Works, pp. 237–258.

Gambaro, L., Stewart, K. and Waldfogel, J. (2013) *A Question of Quality: Do Children from Disadvantaged Backgrounds Receive Lower Quality Early Years Education and Care in England?* London: London School of Economics. Available at: http://eprints.lse.ac.uk/51274/1/__Libfile_repository_Content_Waldfogel,%20J_Waldfogel_Question_quality_children_2013.pdf (accessed 1 May 2015).

Garvey, D. and Lancaster, A. (2010) *Leadership for Quality in Early Years and Playwork*. London: National Children's Bureau.

Georgeson, J. and Campbell-Barr, V. (2015) 'Pulling the threads together', in V. Campbell-Barr and J. Georgeson (eds), *International Perspectives on Early Years Workforce Development*. Northwich: Critical Publishing, pp. 136–42.

Georgeson, J., Campbell-Barr, V., Mathers, S. with Boag-Munroe, G., Parker-Rees, R. and Caruso, F. (2014) *Two-Year-Olds in England: An Exploratory Study*. Available at: http://tactyc.org.uk/wp-content/uploads/2014/11/TACTYC_2_year_olds_Report_2014.pdf (accessed 1 May 2015).

Ghaye, A. and Ghaye, K. (1998) *Teaching and Learning through Critical Reflective Practice*. Trowbridge: David Fulton.

Gibbs, G. (1988) *Learning by Doing: A Guide to Teaching and Learning Methods*. London: Further Education Unit.

Gilroy, P. and Wilcox, B. (1997) 'Ofsted, criteria and the nature of social understanding: a Wittgensteinian critique of the practice of educational judgement', *British Journal of Educational Studies*, 45 (1): 22–38.

Goleman, D., Boyatzis, R. and McKee, A. (2002) *The New Leaders*. London: Little Brown.

Goodfellow, J. (2005) 'Market childcare: preliminary considerations of a "property view" of the child', *Contemporary Issues in Early Childhood*, 6 (1): 54–65.

Grammatikopoulos, V., Gregoriadis, A., Tsigilis, N. and Zachopoulou, E. (2014) 'Parental conceptions of quality in Greek early childhood education', *European Early Childhood Education Research Journal*, 22 (1): 134–48.

Greenfield, S. (2012) 'Nursery home visits: rhetoric and realities', *Journal of Early Childhood Research*, 10 (1): 100–12.

Hadfield, M., Jopling, M., Needham, M., Waller, T., Coleyshaw, L., Emira, M. and Royle, K. (2010) *Longitudinal Study of Early Years Professional Status: An Exploration of Progress, Leadership and Impact – Final Report*. Wolverhampton: University of Wolverhampton.

Hall, V. (1996) *Dancing on the Ceiling: A Study of Women Managers in Education*. London: SAGE.

Hard, L. M. and O'Gorman, L. M. (2007) '"Push-me" or "Pull-you"? An opportunity for early childhood leadership in the implementation of Queensland's early years curriculum', *Contemporary Issues in Early Childhood*, 8 (1): 50–60.

Harper, D. (2008) 'Towards a theory of entrepreneurial teams', *Journal of Business Venturing*, 23: 613–26.

Harwood, D., Klopper, A., Osanyin, A. and Vanderlee, M. (2013) '"It's more than care": early childhood educators' concepts of professionalism', *Early Years: An International Research Journal*, 33 (1): 4–17.

Hayes, C., Daly, J., Duncan, M., Gill, R. and Whitehouse, A. (2014) *Developing as a Reflective Early Years Professional: A Thematic Approach*. Northwich: Critical Publishing.

Heckman, J. (2000) *Invest in the Very Young*. Chicago, IL: Ounce of Prevention Fund and the University of Chicago Harris School of Public Policy Studies. Available at: www.montanakidscount.com/fileaccess/getfile/20.pdf (accessed 15 October 2015)

Heikka, J. and Waniganayake, M. (2011) 'Pedagogical leadership from a distributed perspective within the context of early childhood education', *International Journal of Leadership in Education: Theory and Practice*, 14 (4): 499–512.

Hendrick, H. (1997) 'Constructions and reconstructions of British childhood: an interpretative survey, 1800 to the present', in A. James and A. Prout (eds), *Constructing and Reconstructing Childhood: Contemporary Issues in the Sociological Study of Childhood*. London: RoutledgeFalmer, pp. 34–62.

Hersey, P. and Blanchard, K. H. (1977) *Management of Organizational Behavior* (3rd edition). Englewood Cliffs, NJ: Prentice-Hall.

Ho, C. W. D. (2008) 'Exploring the definitions of quality early childhood programmes in a market-driven context: case studies of two Hong Kong pre-schools', *International Journal of Early Years Education*, 16 (3): 223–36.

Ho, D. (2012) 'The paradox of power in leadership in early childhood education', *Peabody Journal of Education: Issues of Leadership, Policy, and Organizations*, 87 (2): 253–66.

Hochschild, A. R. (1983) *The Managed Heart: Commercialisation of Human Feeling* (3rd edition). Berkeley, CA: University of California Press.

Hodkinson, P. (2004) 'Research as a form of work: expertise, community and methodological objectivity', *British Educational Research Journal*, 30 (1): 9–26.

Hopkins, R., Stokes, L. and Wilkinson, D. (2010) *Quality, Outcomes and Costs in Early Years Education*. London: National Institute of Economic and Social Research. Available at: http://niesr.ac.uk/sites/default/files/publications/Quality%20Outcomes%20and%20Costs%20in%20early%20Years%20Education.pdf (accessed 30 April 2015).

Huskins, T., Kostadintcheva, K., Greevy, H., Salmon, C., Dobie, S., Medien., K., with Littlewood, M. and D'Souza, J. (2014) *The Childcare and Early Years Survey of Parents 2012–2013*. London: Department for Education. Available at: www.gov.uk/government/uploads/system/uploads/attachment_data/file/275992/SFR06-2014_ Childcare_and_Early_Years_Survey_of_Parents_2012-13_final.pdf (accessed 20 April 2015).

James, A. and Prout, A. (1997) *Constructing and Reconstructing Childhood: Contemporary Issues in the Sociological Study of Childhood*. London: RoutledgeFalmer.

James, W. (1892) *The Stream of Consciousness*. Available at: http://psychclassics.yorku.ca/James/jimmy11.htm (accessed 15 February 2015).

Jenks, C. (2004) 'Constructing childhood sociologically', in M. J. Kehily (ed.), *An Introduction to Childhood Studies*. Maidenhead: Open University Press/McGraw-Hill, pp. 77–95.

Johns, C. (2009) *Becoming a Reflective Practitioner*. Chichester: Wiley.

Jones, C. and Pound, L. (2008) *Leadership and Management in the Early Years: From Principles to Practice*. Maidenhead: Open University Press.

Jones, P. (2014) 'Training and workforce issues in the early years', in G. Pugh and B. Duffy (eds), *Contemporary Issues in the Early Years* (6th edition). London: SAGE, pp. 255–72.

Karp, T. and Helgo, T. (2008) 'From change management to change leadership: embracing chaotic change in public service organizations', *Journal of Change Management*, 8 (1): 85–96.

Keely, B. (2008) *How What You Know Shapes Your Life*. Paris: Organisation for Economic Co-operation and Development (OECD).

Klikauer, T. (2013) *Managerialism: A Critique of an Ideology*. London: Palgrave MacMillan.

Kolb, D. A. (1984) *Experiential Learning: Experience as the Source of Learning and Development*. Englewood Cliffs, NJ: Prentice-Hall.

Krieger, J. (2007) 'The political economy of New Labour: the failure of a success story?', *New Political Economy*, 12 (3): 421–32.

Kübler-Ross, E. (1969) *On Death and Dying*. London: Routledge.

Kupers, W. (2007) 'Perspectives on integrating leadership and followership', *International Journal of Leadership Studies*, 2 (3): 194–221.

Ladkins, D. (2013) 'Leading beautifully: how mastery, coherence and purpose contribute to inspirational leadership performance', *Leadership Quarterly*, 19 (1): 31–41.

Lancaster, P. (2002) *Listening to Young Children*. London: National Children's Bureau.

Law, S. and Glover, D. (2000) *Educational Leadership and Learning*. London: Open University Press.

Leeson, C. (2009) 'The involvement of looked after children in making decisions about their present and future care needs'. Unpublished PhD thesis, University of Plymouth.

Leeson, C. (2010) 'Leadership in early childhood settings', in R. Parker-Rees, C. Leeson, J. Willan, J. and J. Savage (eds), *Early Childhood Studies: An Introduction to the Study of Children's Worlds and Children's Lives* (3rd edition). Exeter: Learning Matters, pp. 112–24.

Leeson, C. (2014) 'The pressures of leading early years services in a changing world', in J. Moyles, J. Payler and J. Georgeson (eds), *Early Years Foundations: Critical Issues*. London: Open University Press, pp. 143–54.

Leeson, C., Campbell-Barr, V. and Ho, D. (2012) 'Leading for quality improvement: a comparative research agenda in early childhood education in England and Hong Kong', *International Journal of Leadership in Education*, 15 (2): 221–36.

Lewis, J., Knijn, T., Martin, C. and Ostner, I. (2008) 'Patterns of development in work/family reconciliation policies for parents in France, Germany, the Netherlands, and the UK in the 2000s', *Social Politics: International Studies in Gender, State and Society*, 15 (3): 261–86.

Likert, R. (1967) *The Human Organisation: Its Management and Value*. New York: McGraw-Hill.

Lloyd, E. and Penn, H. (2010) 'Why do childcare markets fail? Comparing England and the Netherlands', *Public Policy Research*, 17 (1): 42–8.

MacNaughton, G. (2005) *Doing Foucault in Early Childhood Studies: Applying Poststructural Ideas*. London: Routledge.

Madrid, S. and Dunn-Kenney, M. (2010) 'Persecutory guilt, surveillance and resistance: the emotional themes of early childhood educators', *Contemporary Issues in Early Childhood*, 11 (4): 388–401.

Mahon, R. and McBride, S. (2009) 'Standardizing and disseminating knowledge: the role of the OECD in global governance', *European Political Science Review*, 1 (1): 83–101.

Mann, S. (2004) '"People-work": emotion management, stress and coping', *British Journal of Guidance and Counselling*, 32 (2): 205–21.

Marinova, S., Moon, H. and Kamdar, D. (2013) 'Getting ahead or getting along? The two-facet conceptualization of conscientiousness and leadership emergence', *Organization Science*, 24 (4): 1257–76.

Mason, J. (2002) *Researching Your Own Practice: The Discipline of Noticing*. London: RoutledgeFalmer.

Mathers, S., Singler, R. and Karemaker, A. (2012) *Improving Quality in the Early Years: A Comparison of Perspectives and Measures*. Oxford/London. Available at: www.education.ox.ac.uk/research/fell/research/improving-quality-in-the-early-years/ (accessed 1 May 2015).

Mathers, S., Ranns, H., Karemaker, A., Moody, A., Sylva, K., Graham, J. and Siraj-Blatchford, I. (2011) *Evaluation of Graduate Leaders Fund*. London: Department for Education, Dfe-RR144.

Matthews, P. and Sammons, P. (2004) *Improvement through Inspection: An Evaluation of the Impact of Ofsted's Work*. London: Ofsted/Crown.

McBride, P. and Maitland, S. (2002) *Putting Emotional Intelligence into Practice*. London: McGraw-Hill.

McDowall Clark, R. and Baylis, S. (2012) '"Wasted down there": policy and practice with the under-threes', *Early Years: An International Research Journal*, 32 (2): 229–42.

McDowall Clark, R. and Murray, J. (2012) *Reconceptualising Leadership in the Early Years*. London: Open University Press.

McEldowney, R., Bobrowski, P. and Granberg, A. (2009) 'Factors affecting the next generation of women leaders: mapping the challenges, antecedents and consequences of leadership', *Journal of Leadership Studies*, 3 (2): 24–30.

McGillivray, G. (2008) 'Nannies, nursery nurses and early years professionals: constructions of professional identity in the early years workforce in England', *European Early Childhood Education Research Journal*, 16 (2): 242–54.

Melhuish, E. C. (2004) *A Literature Review of the Impact of Early Years Provision on Young Children, with Emphasis Given to Children from Disadvantaged Backgrounds*. Prepared for the National Audit Office by the Institute for the Study of Children, Families and Social Issues, Birkbeck, University of London.

Metcalfe, B. and Metcalfe, J. (2008) *Engaging Leadership: Creating Organisations that Maximise the Potential of Their People*. London: Chartered Institute of Personnel and Development.

Mitchell, L. (2010) 'Construction of childhood in early childhood education policy debate in New Zealand', *Contemporary Issues in Early Childhood*, 11 (4): 328–41.

Mooney, A. and Blackburn, T. (2003) *Children's Views on Childcare Quality*. London: Department for Education and Skills.

Moss, P. (2006) 'From childcare to a pedagogical discourse: or putting care in its place', in J. Lewis (ed.), *Children, Changing Families and Welfare States*. Cheltenham: Edward Elgar, pp. 154–72.

Moss, P. (2014) 'Early childhood policy in England 1997–2013: anatomy of a missed opportunity', *International Journal of Early Years Education*, 22 (4): 346–58.

Moss, P. and Penn, H. (1996) *Transforming Nursery Education*. London: Paul Chapman.

Moyles, J. (2001) 'Passion, paradox and professionalism in the early years', *Early Years*, 21 (2): 81–95.

Moyles, J. (2006) *Effective Leadership and Management in the Early Years*. Maidenhead: Open University Press/McGraw-Hill Education.

Moyles, J., Adams, S. and Musgrove, A. (2002) *SPEEL: Study of Pedagogical Effectiveness*. London: Department for Education and Skills.

Muijs, D., Aubrey, C., Harris, A. and Briggs, M. (2004) 'How do they manage? A review of the research on leadership in early childhood', *Journal of Early Childhood Research*, 2 (2): 157–60.

Munton, T., Mooney, A., Moss, P., Petrie, P., Clark, A. and Woolner, J. (2002) *Research on Ratios, Group Size and Staff Qualifications and Training in Early Years and Childcare Settings*. Research Report No. 320. London: Thomas Coram Research Unit, Institute of Education, University of London.

Murray, J. and McDowall Clark, R. (2013) 'Reframing leadership as a participative pedagogy: the working theories of early years professionals', *Early Years: An International Research Journal*, 33 (3): 289–301.

National College of School Leadership (NCSL) (2004) *National Professional Qualification in Integrated Centre Leadership*. Nottingham: NCSL.

National College of Teaching and Learning (NCTL) (2013) *Teachers Standards Early Years*, Available at: www.gov.uk/government/publications (accessed 12 January 2015).

Neugebauer, R. (1985) 'Are you an effective leader?', *Child Care Information Exchange*, 46: 18–26.

Neuman, M. J. (2005) 'Governance of early childhood education and care: recent developments in OECD countries', *Early Years*, 25 (2): 129–41.

Neville, S. (2013) *'More Great Childcare': An Analysis of the Government's Plans Written by Childminders*. Available at: www.childmindersforum.co.uk and www.bestbear.co.uk/resources/documents/childminding-forum-response-to-more-great-childcare.pdf (accessed 10 January 2014).

Nias, J., Southworth, G. and Yeomans, R. (1989) *Staff Relationships in the Primary School*. London: Cassell.

Northouse, P. G. (2010) *Leadership: Theory and Practice* (5th edition). London: SAGE.

Nutbrown, C. (2012) *Foundations for Quality: The Independent Review of Early Education and Childcare Qualifications – Final Report*. Runcorn: Department for Education.

OECD (no date) *The Organisation for Economic Co-operation and Development (OECD)*. Available at: www.oecd.org/about/ (accessed 29 April 2015).

OECD (2001) *Starting Strong: Early Childhood Education and Care*. Paris: OECD.

OECD (2006) *Starting Strong II: Early Childhood Education and Care*. Paris: OECD.

OECD (2011) *Starting Strong III: A Quality Toolbox for Early Childhood Education and Care*. Paris: OECD.

OECD (2015) *Starting Strong IV: Monitoring Quality in Early Childhood Education and Care*. Paris: OECD.

Office for Standards in Education (Ofsted) (2014) *Are You Ready? Good Practice in School Readiness*. London: Ofsted.

Osgood, J. (2004) 'Time to get down to business?', *Journal of Early Childhood Research*, 2 (1): 5–24.

Osgood, J. (2006) 'Professionalism and performativity: the feminist challenge facing early years practitioners', *Early Years: An International Journal of Research and Development*, 26 (2): 187–99.

Osgood, J. (2012) *Narratives from the Nursery: Negotiating the Professional Identities in Early Childhood*. Abingdon: Routledge.

Owen, H. (2000) *In Search of Leaders*. Chichester: Wiley.

Payler, J. and Georgeson, J. (2014) 'Qualifications and quality in the early years foundation stage', in J. Moyles, J. Payler and J. Georgeson (eds), *Early Years Foundations: Critical Issues*. Maindenhead: McGraw-Hill Education, pp. 52–64.

Pedler, M., Burgoyne, J. and Boydell, T. (2004) *Managers' Guide to Leadership*. London: McGraw-Hill.

Pemberton, S. (2006) 'Quietly far reaching: the influence of the mentor during the first year of the NPQICL Rollout 2005/2006' (unpublished Master's dissertation, Pen Green Leadership Centre).

Penn, H. (2010) 'Shaping the future: how human capital arguments about investment in early childhood are being (mis)used in poor countries', in N. Yelland (ed.), *Contemporary Perspective on Early Childhood Education*. Maidenhead: Open University Press, pp. 49–65.

Penn, H. (2011a) 'Gambling on the market: the role of for-profit provision in early childhood education and care', *Journal of Early Childhood Research*, 9 (2): 150–61.

Penn, H. (2011b) *Quality in Early Childhood Services*. Maidenhead: McGraw-Hill.

Pound, L. (2011) *Influencing Early Childhood Education: Key Figures, Philosophies and Ideas*. Maidenhead: McGraw-Hill/Open University Press.

Ransom, H. (2013) *'More Great Childcare': Survey of NCB Early Years Networks*. London: National Children's Bureau.

Roberts-Holmes, G. (2014) 'The "datafication" of early years pedagogy: "if the teaching is good, the data should be good and if there's bad teaching, there is bad data"', *Journal of Education Policy*, 30 (3): 1–13.

Rodd, J. (1998) *Leadership in Early Childhood: The Pathway to Professionalism* (2nd edition). Sydney: Allen and Unwin.

Rodd, J. (2006) *Leadership in Early Childhood* (3rd edition). Buckingham: Open University Press.

Rodd, J. (2012) *Leadership in Early Childhood: The Pathway to Professionalism* (4th edition). Buckingham: Open University Press.

Rogers, C. (1951) *Client-Centered Therapy: Its Current Practice, Implications and Theory*. London: Constable.

Rosenthal, L. (2004) 'Do school inspections improve school quality? Ofsted inspections and school examination results in the UK', *Economics of Education Review*, 23 (2): 143–51.

Rosenthal, M. K. (2003) 'Quality in early childhood education and care: a cultural context', *European Early Childhood Education Research Journal*, 11 (2): 101–16.

Royston, S. and Rodrigues, L. (2013) *Breaking Barriers: How to Help Children's Centres Reach Disadvantaged Families*. London: The Children's Society [online]. Available at: www.childrenssociety.org.uk/sites/default/files/tcs/breaking_barriers_report.pdf (accessed 1 October 2013).

Ruch, G. (2002) 'From triangle to spiral: reflective practice in social work education, practice and research', *Social Work Education*, 21 (2): 199–216.

Saltiel, D. (2003) 'Teaching research and practice on a post qualifying child care programme', *Social Work Education*, 22 (1): 105–11.

Sammons, P., Sylva, K., Melhuish, E. C., Siraj-Blatchford, I., Taggart, B., Toth, K. and Smees, R. (2014) *Influences on Students' GCSE Attainment and Progress at Age 16: Effective Pre-school, Primary and Secondary Education 3–16 Project (EPPSE 3–16)*. London: Institute of Education and Department for Education. Available at: www.gov.uk/government/uploads/system/uploads/

attachment_data/file/351496/RR354_-_Students__educational_and_developmental_outcomes_at_age_16.pdf (accessed 1 May 2015).

Schön, D. (1983) *The Reflective Practitioner*. New York: Basic Books.

Selbie, P., Blakemore, L., Farley, C. and Campbell-Barr, V. (2015) 'Britain: a complex mix of philosophy and politics', in V. Campbell-Barr and J. Georgeson (eds), *International Perspectives on Early Years Workforce Development*. Northwich: Critical Publishing, pp. 14–26.

Sheppard, M. (1995) *Care Management and the New Social Work: A Critical Analysis*. London: Whiting & Birch.

Sinclair, R. (2004) 'Participation in practice: making it meaningful, effective and sustainable', *Children and Society*, 18 (2): 106–18.

Siraj-Blatchford, I. and Manni, L. (2007) *Effective Leadership in the Early Years Sector: The ELEYS Study (Issues in Practice)*. London: Institute of Education.

Smith, P. (1992) *Emotional Labour of Nursing*. Basingstoke: Macmillan.

Solly, K. (2003) 'What do early childhood leaders do to maintain and enhance the significance of the early years?', Paper presented at the Institute of Education, University of London, 22 May.

Sommer, D., Pramling Samuelsson, I. and Hundeide, K. (2013) 'Early childhood care and education: a child perspective paradigm', *European Early Childhood Education Research Journal*, 21 (4): 459–75.

Spencer, B. and Dubiel, J. (2013) 'Inspecting and evaluating the quality and standards of early years and childcare provision', in G. Pugh and B. Duffy (eds), *Contemporary Issues in the Early Years* (6th edition). London: SAGE, pp. 73–88.

Stroebe, M. S. and Schut, H. (1999) 'The Dual Process Model of coping with bereavement: rationale and description', *Death Studies*, 23 (3): 197–224.

Sumsion, J. (2006) 'The corporatization of Australian childcare: towards an ethical audit and research agenda', *Journal of Childhood Research*, 4 (2): 99–120.

Syed, J. (2008) 'From transgression to suppression: implications of moral values and societal norms on emotional labour', *Gender, Work and Organisation*, 15 (2): 185–201.

Sylva, K., Siraj-Blatchford, I. and Taggart, B. (2010) *Early Childhood Environment Rating Scale Extension to ECERS-E*. London: Trentham Books.

Sylva, K., Melhuish, E., Sammons, P., Siraj-Blatchford, I. and Taggart, B. (2004) *The Effective Provision of Pre-school Education (EPPE) Project: Final Report – A Longitudinal Study Funded by the DfES 1997–2004*. London: Institute of Education, University of London/Department for Education and Skills/Sure Start.

Sylva, K., Melhuish, E., Sammons, P., Siraj-Blatchford, I. and Taggart, B. with Smees, R., Welcomme, W. and Hollingworth, K. (2014) *Students' Educational and Developmental Outcomes at Age 16: Effective Pre-School, Primary and Secondary Education (EPPSE 3-16) Project*. London: Department for Education.

Taggart, G. (2011) 'Don't we care? The ethics and emotional labour of early years professionalism', *Early Years: An International Research Journal*, 31 (1): 85–95.

Tannenbaum, R. and Schmidt, W. (1958) 'How to choose a leadership pattern', *Harvard Business Review*, 36 (2): 95–101.
Tanner, E., Welsh, E. and Lewis, J. (2006) 'The quality-defining process in early years services: a case study', *Children & Society*, 20 (1): 4–16.
Teaching Agency (TA) (2013) *Teacher Standards (Early Years)*. London: Teaching Agency.
Telford, H. (1996) *Transforming Schools through Collaborative Leadership*. London: Falmer Press.
Tobin, J. (2005) 'Quality in early childhood education: an anthropologist's perspective', *Early Education and Development*, 16 (4): 421–34.
Torrance, D. (2013) 'Distributed leadership: challenging five generally held assumptions', *School Leadership & Management: Formerly School Organisation*, 33 (4): 354–72.
Tuckman, B. (1965) 'Developmental sequence in small groups', *Psychological Bulletin*, 63 (6): 384–99.
Urban, M. (2008) 'Dealing with uncertainty: challenges and possibilities for the early childhood profession', *European Early Childhood Education Research Journal*, 16 (2): 135–52.
Vecchio, R. (2003) 'Entrepreneurship and leadership: common trends and common threads', *Human Resource Management Review*, 13: 303–27.
Vincent, C., Braun, A. and Ball, S. J. (2008) 'Childcare, choice and social class: caring for young children in the UK', *Critical Social Policy*, 28 (1): 5–26.
West-Burnham, J., Farrar, M. and Otero, G. (2007) *Schools and Communities: Working Together to Transform Children's Lives*. London: Network Continuum.
Whalley, M. (2006) 'Leadership in integrated centres and services for children and families: a community development approach – engaging with the struggle', *Childrenz Issues: Journal of the Children's Issues Centre*, 10 (2): 8–13.
Wickett, K. and Selbie, P. (2015) 'Providing an enabling environment', in R. Parker-Rees and C. Leeson (eds), *Early Childhood Studies: An Introduction to the Study of Children's Worlds and Children's Lives* (4th edition). London: SAGE pp. 85–98.
Wincott, D. (2004) *Devolution, Social Democracy and Policy Diversity in Britain: The Case of Childcare and Early Years Policies*. Available at: www.ippr.org/assscts/media/uploadedFiles/ipprnorth/events/2004/sem1-paper%20on%20childcare.pdf (accessed 14 August 2014).
Woodrow, C. and Busch, G. (2008) 'Repositioning early childhood leadership as action and activism', *Early Childhood Education Research Journal*, 16 (1): 83–93.
Wright, L. (2008) 'Merits and limitations of distributed leadership: experiences and understandings of school principals', *Canadian Journal of Educational Administration and Policy*, 69: 1–33.

INDEX

accountability
  to children, 66–68
  critical role of leaders and, 63–66, *64*
  definition of, 135
  internal accountability, 74–76
  to parents and families, 68–69
  to team, 69–70
  top-down accountabilities, 70–74
action-centred leadership, 56
Adair, J., 56
Alexander, E., 32, 33
attachment theories, 16
Attard, K., 106
Aubrey, C., 57

Bernstein, P., 22
Blackburn, T., 41
Blanchard, K. H., 53, 54
Bourdieu, P., 106
Brayfield, A., 37
Bronfenbrenner, U., 65

Campbell-Barr, V., 32, 58, 97
Carter Dillon, R., 19, 20
case study practitioners
  characteristics of, 83–85
  on quality, 89–103
  writing framework and, 86–87
  See also specific practitioners
Chemers, M. M., 54
Cheryl (case study practitioner), 84, 101–103, 120–122, 123–124
chief executives, 77
Childcare and Early Years Survey of Parents, 37–38
Children Act (2004), 66, 71
children's needs, 101–103
children's rights, 96–97
Clark, A., 67–68
Cleveland, G., 40

Coker, C., 124
Coleyshaw, J., 41
Common Assessment Framework (CAF), 66
contingency theories of leadership, 53–55
Cottle, M., 32, 33
Crawford, M., 105–106

Dahlberg, G., 19, 35–36, 81
discourses, 24–25, 135
distributed leadership, **51**, 56–58
Douglass, A., 115

early childhood education and care (ECEC), use of term, 14
Early Childhood Environment Rating Scale (ECERS), 23–25, 30, 31, 33
Early Childhood Environment Rating Scale- Extension (ECERS-E), 31
Early Childhood Environment Rating Scale-Revised (ECERS-R), 31
Early Years Educators, 107
Early Years Foundation Stage (EYFS), 2–3, 15, 66, 96–97
early years leaders
  accountabilities of, 63–76
  as activist leaders, 80–81
  jobs of, *78*, 80
  titles of, 76–80, *78*
  See also leadership
Early Years Professionals (EYPs), 77, 100, 107
early years services
  cultural interpretations of, 21–22
  hegemonic views of, 19–21
Early Years Teachers (EYTs), 77, 100, 107
Ebbeck, M., 30
educare, 15, 49, 135
Effective Pre-School, Primary and Secondary Education (EPPSE) Report, 107
Effective Provision of Pre-school Education (EPPE) project, 18–19, 24–25, 33

Eisenstadt, N., 94
Elliott, I., 124
emotional labour, 74–76, 123–124
emotional well-being, 110–114, 124–125
emotionology, 74–76, 135
entrepreneurial leadership, **51**, 58–60
entrepreneurial teams, **51**
Eraut, M., 101
European Union (EU), 15–16
Every Child Matters (DfES, 2004), 40–41, 66

families. *See* parents and families
Fenech, M., 32
Fiedler, F. E., 54
Foucault, M., 34–35
Freire, P., 121

Garvey, D., 79
Georgeson, J., 31–32, 98, 99–100
Ghaye, A., 125
Ghaye, K., 125
Gibbs, G., 108
Gittell, J., 115
global knowledge economy, 17–19
Graduate Leader Fund, 73
Greenfield, S., 115

Hall, V., 77, 78
Hayes, C., 107
Heckman, J., 17–18
Heikka, J., 50
heroic leadership, 50, **51**
Hersey, P., 53, 54
hierarchy of needs, 56
Ho, D., 57
Hopkins, R., 31
human capital theory, 17–19, 20, 22, 23, 35, 135
Huskins, T., 36–37

Infant and Toddler Environment Rating Scale (ITERS), 31

Jacky (case study practitioner), 84, 90–93, 97, 99, 110–114, 124, 125
Johns, C., 125
Jones, P., 100

Kolb, D. A., 108
Korintus, M., 37

Lancaster, A., 79
language, 92–93
leadership
 bricolage approach to, 60–61
 emotional well-being and, 110–114

leadership *cont.*
 history of, 48–50
 importance of, 1–2, 47–48
 managerialism and, 32–33
 theories on, 50–60, **51**
 See also early years leaders; reflection and reflexivity
Leeson, C., 50, 59
Likert, R., 53–54

MacNaughton, G., 25, 107
Mahon, R., 14
Malaguzzi, L., 36
managerialism, 32–33, 49, 58, 135
managers, 77–80, *78*
Maslow, A., 56
maternal care, 16
Mathers, S., 23–24, 31, 33, 36–37
Matthews, P., 30
McBride, S., 14
McDowall Clark, R., 69–70
McGillivray, G., 33
Meeting the Childcare Challenge (DfEE, 1998), 14–15
modernity and modernism
 definition of, 136
 leadership and, 52–56, 58–61, 73
 quality and, 22–25, 32, 34, 42, 72–73, 123, 128–129
Mooney, A., 41
More Great Childcare (DfE, 2013), 15, 64, 93–94
Mosaic Approach, 67–68
Moss, P., 14, 19, 35–36, 67–68, 81
motivational theory, 56
Moyles, J., 32
Munton, T., 93
Murray, J., 69–70

National Childcare Strategy, 14–15, 39
National Institute of Child Health and Human Development (NICHD), 16–17
National Professional Qualification in Integrated Centre Leadership (NPQICL), 55, 107
neo-liberalism, 39–40, 49, 136
Neugebauer, R., 55
Nias, J., 56
Nurseries and Child-Minders Regulations Act (1948), 29

Office for Standards in Education (Ofsted)
 inspection process of, 29–32, 67, 72, 90–93, 97, 99
 panoptic gaze and, 64, 92–93
 parents and, 30, 37
 self-evaluation form and, 67, 91

Organisation for Economic Co-operation and Development (OECD), 13–14
Osgood, J., 33, 58

panoptic gaze
　accountability and, 70–71
　definition of, 136
　leadership and, 60
　Ofsted and, 64, 92–93
　post-structuralism on, 34–36, 56
paradigms, 136
parents and families
　accountability and, 68–69
　choice of childcare services and, 38–40
　partnership with, 114–117, 123
　on quality, 30, 36–40
Pedler, M., 77
Pen Green Leadership Centre, 55
Penn, H., 19, 20
playgroup supervisors, 77
post-modernism, 25, 34
post-structuralism
　definition of, 136
　language and, 92–93
　leadership and, 59–60, 80–81
　on panoptic gaze, 34–36, 56
　quality and, 2, 25–26, 42, 128–129
　reflection and, 106–107
pre-school supervisors, 77
private, voluntary, independent (PVI) sector, 3–4
process quality, 23, 93–97, 136
psychology, 16–17, 21–22

qualifications, 98–99, 100–101
quality
　case study practitioners on, 89–103
　child views on, 40–41
　features of, 42–44, *43*
　global and European interests in, 11–16, 19–20
　importance of, 1–2
　modernist approaches to, 22–25
　outside the rating scales box, 32–34
　parental perspectives on, 36–40
　post-structuralist approaches to, 2, 25–26, 42
　as social investment, 16–19
quality frameworks, 28–32

randomised controlled trials, 23
reflection and reflexivity
　emotional well-being and, 110–114, 124–125
　models of, 108–110

reflection and reflexivity *cont.*
　partnership with parents and, 114–117, 123
　role and importance of, 105–108, 125–126
　teams and, 120–122, 123–124
　themes in, 122–125
　visual maps and, 117–119, *120*
Reggio Emilia approach, 36
Roberts-Holmes, G., 97
Rodd, J., 55
Rosenthal, L., 31
Rosenthal, M. K., 21

Sammons, P., 30
Sandra (case study practitioner), 84, 98–100, 114–117, 124
Santos, B. de S., 20
Schmidt, W., 53, 54–55
Schön, D., 110–111, 124
Selbie, P., 98, 103
self-evaluation form (SEF), 67, 91
situational theories of leadership, 53–55
social agency, 36, 41, 66–67, 95–96, 136
social constructionism, 2
social investment, 16–19, 136
sociology of childhood, 96–97
Solly, K., 78
staffing, 98–100
structural quality, 23, 93–97, 136
style theories of leadership, **51**, 52–53
Sue (case study practitioner), 84, 94–97, 98, 117–119, *120*, 123–124
supranational organisations, 12–14, 19–21, 74, 136

Tannenbaum, R., 53, 54–55
teams
　accountability to, 69–70
　reflection and, 120–122, 123–124
Torrance, D., 57
trait theories of leadership, **51**, 52–53
transactional leadership, 50–52, **51**
transformational leadership, 50, **51**, 56, 59, 124
Tuckman, B., 110

Vincent, C., 37–38
visual maps, 117–119, *120*

Waniganayake, M., 30, 50
Wickett, K., 103
World Bank, 20
Wright, L., 57–58